LIVING WITH THE LIVING DEAD

LIVING WITH THE LIVING DEAD

The Wisdom of the Zombie Apocalypse

GREG GARRETT

OXFORD

UNIVERSITY PRESS

Oxford University Press is a department of the University of Oxford.
It furthers the University's objective of excellence in research, scholarship,
and education by publishing worldwide.Oxford is a registered trade mark of
Oxford University Press in the UK and certain other countries.

Published in the United States of America by Oxford University Press
198 Madison Avenue, New York, NY 10016, United States of America.

CIP data is on file at the Library of Congress.

ISBN 978-0-19-026045-3

1 3 5 7 9 8 6 4 2

Printed by Edwards Brothers Malloy, United States of America

This shall be the plague with which the LORD will strike all the peoples that wage war against Jerusalem: their flesh shall rot while they are still on their feet; their eyes shall rot in their sockets, and their tongues shall rot in their mouths. On that day a great panic from the LORD shall fall on them, so that each will seize the hand of a neighbor, and the hand of the one will be raised against the hand of the other.

—ZECHARIAH 14:12–13 (NRSV)

He has opened the grave, He has unsealed the crypt, He has turned the dead from their black tombs—and set them upon us!

—RICHARD MATHESON, *I Am Legend*

For Terry Nathan,
who made this book possible

CONTENTS

Gallery appears after page 118.

LIVING WITH THE LIVING DEAD

INTRODUCTION

Raising the Dead

It's not rabies. It's a Zombie Apocalypse.
> —DILTON, *Afterlife with Archie*

When it was light enough to use the binoculars he glassed the valley below. Everything paling away into the murk. The soft ash blowing in loose swirls over the blacktop. He studied what he could see. The segments of road down there among the dead trees. Looking for anything of color. Any movement. Any trace of standing smoke.
> —CORMAC MCCARTHY, *The Road*

WINTER IS COMING: THE ZOMBIE APOCALYPSE

It's the end of the world—and who is left? A handful of human survivors wander the landscape. Maybe they're pushing grocery carts or lugging all they possess in backpacks. Whatever direction you look, the countryside is blasted and desolate. Nature has begun to take back what humankind had seized from it over the course of hundreds of years. Grass sprouts through cracks in pavement and asphalt; vines begin to overrun abandoned cars and sprout from derelict buildings. No planes fly overhead, no trains whistle in the lonesome distance. Maybe there's still gasoline that can be siphoned from the occasional gas tank here or there, but cars and trucks are mostly a thing of the past, metal coffins if you're caught in them, because something pursues the human survivors, something that promises a fate worse than death.

If they catch you, they will kill you, yes.

But in those last moments, you will die knowing that they intend to devour you as well.

The landscape I have described above may be inferred from Cormac McCarthy's Pulitzer Prize–winning literary novel *The Road*, but it is immediately recognizable to even more people as the world of the Zombie Apocalypse. In this dominant twenty-first-century narrative, whether the catalyst for the disaster is scientific, mystical, or completely unknown, society has broken down, civilization persists only in isolated pockets, and danger lurks in the shadows at every moment, a danger that doesn't mind eviscerating and consuming you. It's the world of *Night of the Living Dead*, of *Dawn of the Dead* (original and remake), of *The Walking Dead*, of its prequel *Fear the Walking Dead*, of *I Am Legend*, of *Zombieland* ("the United States of Zombieland"), of *Shaun of the Dead*, of the *Supernatural* season 5 episode "The End," of the game *Dead Rising*.

Maybe the whole world hasn't yet collapsed into ruin. Maybe, in the terms of the best-selling *Zombie Survival Guide*, our story has not yet reached the level of a "Class 4" or "doomsday outbreak."[1] Perhaps it is merely the edge of apocalypse, as opposed to postapocalyptic, as in early episodes of *Fear the Walking Dead*. Perhaps only a small town or remote outpost is suffering through an outbreak of the undead, as in the undead feeding frenzy described in the comic and film *30 Days of Night*, the breakout in the all-American town Riverdale in

Afterlife with Archie, the viral infection in the remote California town of Deer Field in *Scouts Guide to the Zombie Apocalypse,* the rural town of River Grove, Oregon, in the *Supernatural* episode "Croatoan," or the localized waves of zombies attacking in zombie modules of the game *Tour of Duty.*

Perhaps the undead (or "unmentionables") are largely an annoyance for the well-trained adventurer, as in the book and film versions of *Pride and Prejudice and Zombies,* although they have reshaped those in their societies to deal with the threat or die.

Or perhaps, as in the world of Westeros (described in the book and TV series *Game of Thrones*), the dead have not yet swept completely over the living. But winter is coming, and the threat of apocalypse still looms large. Rulers and potential rulers jockey for position, execute rivals, prosecute wars, but their petty machinations all take place against the backdrop of the oncoming night that never ends. This is made obvious at the conclusion of the *Game of Thrones* season 5 episode "Hardhome." After a hard-fought battle, the living dead not only reduce a Wildling village to ruin, but in front of a disbelieving Jon Snow (Kit Harington), the Night's King raises his hands, and all the fallen rise to new life in death. The pretensions of all the humans playing their Game of Thrones are suddenly, painfully, revealed. As the *Atlantic*'s Amy Sullivan writes, "Is it over yet? And by 'it,' I mean all of humanity? There's nothing like a horrifying White Walker infestation and bloodbath to put things in perspective."[2]

What hope is there against an enemy such as this that grows more powerful with every human who falls?

As we say at my house, "I predict disaster."

The Zombie Apocalypse has become one of the most prominent stories we tell in the twentieth-century West. As we will understand in this book, it was introduced to our culture beginning with George Romero's seminal movie *The Night of the Living Dead* (1968) and its sequels, before exploding into both popular and cult movies like *Resident Evil, 28 Days Later, Shaun of the Dead, Planet Terror, Zombieland, I Am Legend,* and *World War Z.* The Zombie Apocalypse is the controlling narrative behind the worldwide TV phenomenon *The Walking Dead,* four times (as of 2016) the most popular show in the world among adults aged eighteen to forty-nine. The Zombie Apocalypse narrative shapes blockbuster games such as *Tour of Duty, Diablo III, Dead Rising, Resident Evil,* and *The Walking Dead* and comics like *Marvel Zombies, Afterlife with Archie,* and DC Comics' *Blackest Night* comic event. ("Across the universe, the dead will rise.") This narrative is even the basis for the anticipated future explored in *The Zombie Survival Guide,* a "nonfiction" handbook educating its readers about zombies and how best to survive their depredations. In stories, songs, games, apps, products, and comic events, the Zombie Apocalypse represents one of the most important motifs in contemporary culture.

Across all these platforms, this book explores a common story: the world faces an impending or actual breakdown of society because of creatures that are spreading across the earth, killing everyone in their path or turning them into beings like themselves. Usually these creatures were once human beings but are no longer; they have been altered by a virus, a supernatural agency, science, or some other factor into creatures that cannot help but feed on us. Generally these narratives follow a hero or small group of comrades trying to remain alive and uninfected and in the course of telling their stories also explore the ethical challenges that come with trying to survive in a world come unhinged.

The threats preying on human life in these tales are not always zombies as classically defined in the Romero mythos: corpses returned to some sort of life to feed on the living. Richard Matheson's *I Am Legend* (a primary source for Romero's *Night of the Living Dead*) and later film adaptations center on vampire-like creatures created by a pandemic. Justin Cronin writes about science-spawned vampires who overrun the world in *The Passage* and its sequels *The Twelve* and *City of Mirrors*, and Bram Stoker vampires stalk the inhabitants of a small Alaska town in the comic and film *30 Days of Night*. Other sorts of monsters and aliens threaten to overwhelm and assimilate the human race in films such as *The Thing* and *Invasion of the Body-Snatchers* and episodes of *Doctor Who*, *Torchwood*, and *Star Trek*, while humans themselves might be said to be the ravenous monsters who overrun the world in the Mad Max films, *Wall*E*, and other speculative stories of futures in which humans destroy themselves through their own consumption. But whatever the shape of the menace, the shape of the story remains consistent, and these stories wrestle with serious human issues in the course of exploring the means and costs of survival.

Angela Kang, writer and producer of *The Walking Dead* TV series, told me onstage at the Austin Film Festival that her show is not about zombies but about the human survivors. Survival, she said—what people are willing to do to survive and what it costs them—is at the core of the story that has made the show one of the most-watched on the planet. Mark Protosevich, who wrote the Will Smith film version of *I Am Legend*, agreed with Angela: "Zombie stories are survival stories, and they ask the question 'Under these circumstances, why go on?' And in the face of great adversity, they do go on. It's a microcosm of human experience."[3] In addition to "Why go on?" these stories ask other hard questions. What are people willing to do to survive? And what will those choices do to the people forced to make them?

These stories are, as you probably know, on the very edge of what human beings can stand to watch or read. Some of you reading this book are fascinated by zombies not because you enjoy them or even partake of them but because you are mystified by why something so violent, gory, and hard to stomach has become one of the world's most popular stories. Michael O'Sullivan, in his *Washington Post* review of the 2004 remake of *Dawn of the Dead*, captured what some people love—and others hate—about the genre: that it pushes far past the boundary of good taste. He described *Dawn of the Dead* as "one of the nastiest exercises in cinematic story-telling I have had the pleasure to sit through" and explained that by "nasty" he really meant something supremely positive. The movie was, he said "a paradigm of its genre: bloody (and bloody scary), stylish, smart, audacious and edgy, darkly pessimistic yet inflected with touches of deliciously sick humor.... Its sole aim, and one at which it succeeds admirably, is to simultaneously revolt, scare, and delight you."[4] Whether we talk about the original *Night of the Living Dead*, which, as Roger Ebert noted, scared the living daylights out of many children whose parents had left them at theaters for what they thought would be the usual toothless Saturday horror films, or about *The Walking Dead*, which weekly inspires powerful responses across traditional and social media with each zombie attack and human atrocity, or about amazingly popular first-person shooters like the zombie mode of *Call of Duty: Black Ops*, in which players from across the world meet online to graphically dismember oncoming zombies and survive as many waves as possible, part of the appeal is the visceral, the horrifying, and the unspeakable.[5]

Like war stories, like disaster films, like any kind of narrative that revolts and scares yet also delights us, the Zombie Apocalypse offers a laboratory for observing human emotion and experience. Its excess opens up a multitude of responses that don't get explored in the course of our everyday lives, although these same choices lurk underneath the surface of all our lives. It would seem, then, that in its headline for a recent discussion of *The Walking Dead*, the *Atlantic* has it right: "'The Walking Dead,' Like All Zombie Stories: . . . Not about Zombies at All."[6] The story of the Zombie Apocalypse instead is a way that we ask questions about what it means to be human. Along with a healthy dose of fear and excitement, we get our daily requirement of ethical and philosophical reflection, all in the guise of stories about the living dead.

Zombies are popular villains because they have affinities to us yet seem alien. As Kim Paffenroth points out in his study of the films of George Romero, zombies are creatures poised between two states, straddling the line between human and nonhuman and the boundary between living and dead, and there is something familiarly monstrous about this.[7] Zombies are, in fact, scientifically demonstrated to be among the most frightening menaces we could watch, read about, or fight. Masahiro Mori, the robotics researcher, discovered in his research in the 1970s that humans feel increasingly comfortable with robots as they become more human in appearance, until they become too humanoid, at which point the identification becomes a painful one.[8] While Mori says in a recent interview that science seems to be able to quantify this effect, it is an emotional proof as well as a physiological one; we know it because we feel it, not just because our brain waves change when exposed to such creatures: "the brain waves act that way because we feel eerie. It still doesn't explain why we feel eerie to begin with. The uncanny valley relates to various disciplines, including philosophy, psychology, and design, and that is why I think it has generated so much interest."[9] Echoing Mori's word "eerie," Travis Langley notes of this research that creatures that are "eerily human while obviously nonhuman" seem to push all our buttons, and we can see this by noting how zombies reside in what Mori called *bukimi no tani* (the uncanny valley).

On a chart of the uncanny valley, the deepest dip representing close human likeness yet clear difference is where most zombie scholars would locate the zombie. This graphic evidence simply affirms what many of us already understood intuitively, that as Langley says, of all possible menaces, "a zombie will creep us out the most."[10]

The opening credits of the film *World War Z* offer a montage of contemporary problems: overpopulation and overcrowding, traffic jams, epidemics, toxic waste, all intercut with scenes of nature becoming ever more menacing, ending with swarms and feeding frenzies. It visually depicts a jarring and genuinely frightening idea: that nature operates by certain rules, and that we are pushing up against the very boundaries of those rules. In addition to (or perhaps because of) being supremely frightening in their depiction of almost-human monsters, zombies act as symbols for all sorts of free-floating twenty-first-century anxieties, from the spread of Ebola and Zika to the breakdown of the financial markets to changes in gender roles to the menace of global terrorism. While this conclusion may perhaps be startling if you are not a consumer of all things zombie, it is nothing new. As Paffenroth noted in 2005, critics and fans have long known that zombie films can be "serious and thoughtful examinations of ideas," and his book points out Romero's powerful social criticism of American racism, consumerism, and individualism through the medium of zombie stories.[11]

That serious and thoughtful consideration continues today. If you are an American or European troubled by the flood of Syrian refugees, their slow steady advance might bear some of the menace of the inexorable approach of the undead. If you are a white male in the United States or United Kingdom, the steady loss of power and control and the rapidity of change you experience might feel like the relentless bad news of the Zombie Apocalypse. Whether you are concerned about the seemingly unstoppable spread of religious extremism, or by the growing incivility in public life, or by the relentless breakdown of our infrastructure, or by the science of global warming, all of these menaces bear a relationship to the inexorable advance of the Zombie Apocalypse. Even for those of us who toil every day at jobs that never seem to be finished, or that will have to be done and redone for a seeming eternity, the never-ending stream of zombies bears a correspondence to real life.

Essayist and novelist Chuck Klosterman opines that much of modern life, in fact, feels like killing zombies:

> Every zombie war is a war of repetition. It's always a numbers game. And it's more repetitive than complex. In other words, zombie killing is philosophically similar to reading and deleting 400 work e-mails on a Monday morning or filling out paperwork that only generates more paperwork, or following Twitter gossip out of obligation, or performing tedious tasks in which the only true risk is being consumed by the avalanche. The principal downside to any zombie attack is that the zombies will never stop coming; the principal downside to life is that you will never be finished with whatever it is you do.[12]

What is the unfinished business in your life? What is the task that keeps coming, no matter what? For me, the Zombie Apocalypse is doing dishes: at my house, a never-ending stream of dirty dishes have to be rinsed, placed in the dishwasher, removed from the dishwasher, and placed in cabinets, and just when I think they are done, down, they get back up and the whole exercise has to be performed all over again. Every day offers a new battle; every day is the same old thing, and it exhausts me. Thus do zombies come to stand in not only for exotic and world-threatening menaces, but for mundane exertion, the attack of everyday life that paradoxically can be best told by stories about the walking dead.

In his critically acclaimed 2015 novel *The Making of Zombie Wars*, Aleksandar Hemon writes about a mostly failed screenwriter who is transmuting the bizarre events of his life into a script called *Zombie Wars*. As artists good and bad always do, Hemon's protagonist, Joshua Levin, is exploring the issues of his own life and times—the fall of the Twin Towers, George W. Bush and Donald Rumsfeld generating reasons to go to war with Iraq, a father with prostate cancer, a girlfriend who has thrown him out for sleeping with one of his ESL students from Bosnia who has a troubled daughter and a very troubled husband, a PTSD-maimed landlord who takes creepy liberties with Joshua's underwear—through the story he is spinning about a zombie virus spun out of control. At last, he writes himself toward the sort of hopeful resolution he is finding hard to achieve in real life:

> The prison fort is visible on the horizon, its high walls with watchtowers. The people are exhausted, but they know they've almost made it. GUNFIRE in the distance, zombies LOWING.
> LATER

> Major K BANGS at the steel door....There is no re-
> sponse....Major K BANGS again. The peephole slides open.
> A pair of anxious eyes.
> MAJOR K
> We're all human.[13]

Not only is Joshua using zombie narratives to deal with what is in the papers and what is happening right in front of him; clearly Hemon is as well. It is a way to work out his understandings not only of his native Bosnia—Hemon escaped the country just prior to the horrific violence of the 1990s—but also of his new native country, the United States, and city, Chicago. "The zombie trope," he says, gets deployed to help people deal with their anxieties, and it also helps that his is a story that contains and excuses violence. "America," he says, "believes in violence deeply on the political level," citing the nation's Gulf War interventions, while individual Americans like those he has met in Chicago are also drawn to violence: "they really believe that if they are deprived of access to violence, they are deprived of civic agency."[14] Although not a fan of zombie stories per se, Hemon as an artist—like his character Joshua Levin as an artist, if much more consciously—is using the Zombie Apocalypse as a vehicle for self-understanding, and as a prism to better understand the world around him. He is hardly the only one these days; he just happens to be one of the most articulate and aware of what zombies offer him as an artist and thinker.

These symbols and story tropes connected to zombies, initially limited to cult filmgoers and teen thrill seekers, have clearly evolved into a larger societal discourse. They have, as we see here, leaked from low culture—cheaply made B movies—into high culture—literary novels and short stories. And they have traveled much farther than that; as Dan Solomon notes in an interview with *Walking Dead* creator Robert Kirkman, stories like these, which were once considered to be suitable only for adolescents, examples of pure "geek culture," have now gone totally mainstream, shuffling into every segment of society like zombies flooding into a shopping mall.[15] Staid publications for accountants and investors such as the *Financial Times* and the *Economist* have employed zombie metaphors. A February 2009 *Economist* cover referring to the return of economic nationalism depicts a zombie hand breaking through the ground; a 2013 article on private equity firms in the *Economist* observes how "in the unprofitable shadows of the industry, zombies roam.... These firms are the undead: partly sentient...hard to kill off; and ubiquitous." The *Financial Times* has repeatedly reported on Chinese "zombie companies."[16]

Governments and government agencies tell stories of the Zombie Apocalypse in aid of their missions. Fifty cities around the world (including New York, Paris, Hong Kong, Los Angeles, Chicago, and Tokyo) celebrated World Zombie Day in October 2015 to raise money and awareness for world hunger and homelessness. In 2012, the Centers for Disease Control released a Zombie Apocalypse graphic novel and poster series and teased a contemporary zombie plague on social media to draw attention to its government-mandated mission of disaster preparation. For its part, the state of Kansas, anchored securely in the heartland of America, proclaimed October 2015 "Zombie Preparedness Month." Kansas governor Sam Brownback declared at the signing ceremony: "Preparedness is important and that's what we're trying to get people to pay attention to—to get prepared for any natural disaster. And if you're prepared for zombies you're prepared for anything."[17]

Zombies have become normalized in other sectors of the culture as well. The *Huffington Post* operates a "Zombie Apocalypse" portal for related news. Even the venerable *New York Times* goes so far as to describe our current obsession with zombies as a "cultural moment" and demonstrates this interpretation with reference to the pages of the newspaper itself. The *Times* employed the phrase "Zombie Apocalypse" only twice prior to 2006, but in 2012 the phrase "logged 20 appearances—in political columns, in TV coverage and in an article about peanut butter-and-pickle sandwiches."[18]

When the *New York Times*, the great state of Kansas, the Centers for Disease Control, and bankers and accountants worldwide have all adopted a term as a legitimate descriptor, it has made its official entry into our culture. And zombies are indeed everywhere: we encounter them in zombie runs, walks, and pub crawls; in zombie dolls and zombie makeup; as packaged snack foods and in recipes for foods to whip up to eat with your favorite zombie shows; in zombie lottery tickets, such as "The Walking Dead" tickets sold in Texas and other states; in zombie apps, zombie bowties, zombie guitars, and zombie guitar straps. A zombie crèche featuring a zombie Christ child in a small town in Ohio made the national news in 2015, attracting interested observers and shocked detractors alike. Expensive SUVs in suburban parking lots sport back window stickers displaying their families as stick-figure zombies, tallest to smallest. Amazon sells over 800,000 zombie-related products in categories ranging from films to fashion, and the trend seems only to grow in momentum as the world continues to grow more complex and more frightening. Cultural critic and theorist Evan Calder-Williams declares zombies "the nightmare image of the day," and this certainly seems to be true.[19] Wherever we turn, the living dead lurch toward us.

This book seeks to explore the reasons why, exactly, the Zombie Apocalypse has become the dominant nightmare image of our day. Why is it that we are so drawn to these stories of the end of the world, of walking dead, of a fate that we can delay but perhaps cannot escape? How do stories featuring the undead help us to wrestle with our lives and with what may await us after death? And what do the living dead represent that makes them so powerfully symbolic, particularly today, in so many Western nations?

The popularity of zombie narratives suggests that something more important than mere entertainment is going on, although certainly many people consume them purely for entertainment: shows like *The Walking Dead* and *Game of Thrones* are among the most popular across the planet. But if zombies do indeed stand in for a variety of looming threats, then stories about the Zombie Apocalypse must help us to grapple with universal human themes. How do we deal with our fears about famine, pandemics, and global warming, about predictions of the Rapture or of the Mayan end of the world? How do we wrestle with phenomena that seem to be out of our control, such as terrorism, war, and economic uncertainty? A menace that strides inexorably toward us, that seems unstoppable, and yet against which individual human beings seem able to register some small successes may be the perfect villain for the twenty-first century. Zombies can carry the freight of many of these fears and negative emotions, but as Episcopal priest and canon Torey Lightcap points out, popular narratives like *The Walking Dead* also offer us the opportunity to explore other important human themes: "When is a person not a person anymore? What is a soul? Where do we draw the line in doing harm to one another in order to save ourselves? How much stress can we take before we are fundamentally changed in who we are? Does a virus sleeping in our veins mean we deliberately cut off all other access to life around us? And lately the question has been very much along these lines: When does the impulse to protect ourselves mean we transcend mere wagon-circling and instead start actively hurting others?"[20] For those who at the writing of this book are worried about the stream of refugees from the Middle East—or for those following the statements of president-elect Donald J. Trump, including his promise to ban Muslims on account of their fanatical coreligionists who seek to carry out acts of terror—zombie narratives are more than simply fantastic escapes. They symbolize whatever it is that people fear. These stories of the supernatural or of science run amuck are dealing with the very real stuff of modern life.

Although we are not always conscious of doing so, we use stories and symbols from our culture and from our wisdom traditions alike to help us make sense of the world and our place in it. It is one of the most powerful understandings of what we call "myth," not because these stories are false and unprovable, as we usually think of myth, but because in some profound and powerful way, they are unassailably true. As Karen Armstrong notes, "both art and religion try to make some ultimate sense of a flawed and tragic world," and philosopher Eugene Thacker, in his book *In the Dust of This Planet*, expands this reliance on mythology and theology by suggesting that what earlier eras might have understood through other lenses we tend to explore today through tales of supernatural horror.[21] Humans have always sought to make sense of the world, whether through art, mythology, or theology; these tales are simply a contemporary manifestation of a timeless human need: the quest for wisdom and meaning.

In 2013, in the early stages of gathering ideas for this book, I discussed stories of the undead for audiences at the American Library in Paris and at Magdalene College, Cambridge. Members of both audiences independently brought up philosopher Alain de Botton's book *Religion for Atheists*, which explores the universal human need for meaning. They asked whether zombie narratives might in some way be serving the function for their audiences of religions or more formal wisdom traditions. I answered in the affirmative. As de Botton, Richard Dawkins, and other atheists have noted, one does not have to be religious to seek ethical insight, connection, and transcendence, and many readers, gamers, and filmgoers could indeed be exploring universal human themes and needs in their consumption of zombie stories.

In his book, de Botton observes that "one can be left cold by the doctrines of the Christian Trinity and the Buddhist Eightfold Path and yet at the same time be interested in the ways in which religions deliver sermons, promote morality, engender a spirit of community, make use of art and architecture, inspire travels, train minds, and encourage gratitude."[22] Today's millions consuming zombie narratives on TV, in films, and across other platforms are spiritual beings with spiritual needs. Although they may not belong to a formal faith community, stories of the Zombie Apocalypse may be helping to shape and form them. These stories may deliver sermons, promote morality, engender a spirit of community, and offer other spiritual and emotional comfort, so one of the central interests of this book is the ways these stories might form people.

De Botton suggests that two urgent human needs are the making of community—an ever more elusive goal in our wired age—and the development of a framework for the serious consideration of death and suffering. The zombie narrative is particularly strong in both these areas. In these pages, I will not only be sketching the development of the genre and considering societal reasons for its popularity, I will be taking stories of the Zombie Apocalypse seriously as vehicles for meaning and considering what those meanings might be. These stories of the living dead, strangely enough, may be an essential aid to the living, a vital part of achieving comfort, equilibrium, and wisdom for the audiences who consume them, which may explain why artists and storytellers have set the dead walking throughout history when peril has seemed to loom like a creeping cloud over the human race.

A note on methodology and scope: in this work, as in my book on the afterlife, *Entertaining Judgment*, and in most of my writing on art, literature, culture, and meaning, I am offering three different lenses through which readers might look. From my literary training, I try to offer close reading of texts, whether those texts are novels, films, works of art, or other artifacts. In close reading, we are asking the questions "What does this say?" and "How does it say it?" From a cultural and anthropological standpoint, I try to offer cultural criticism of individual works and the larger corpus. Here, we are asking the questions "Why are these works so popular?" and "What needs are being served for their consumers?" And last, through theological and philosophical enquiry, I want to explore ultimate questions about our humanity and about the cosmos we inhabit. In this theological approach, we are asking "What existential questions do these stories consider?" and "In what ways are these stories related to the provisional answers found in scripture and theology?" Because my own formal training is as a Christian theologian, works of the Judeo-Christian tradition are unquestionably privileged here, although I try to present insights from other traditions as well.

The works chosen for inclusion in this book are largely well-known or critically acclaimed versions of the Zombie Apocalypse story. I have tried to circle back to the same narratives throughout so that the uninitiated will develop some anchoring connections to characters, story lines, and themes. Instead of trying to discuss the literally thousands of films, games, novels, comics, apps, and TV episodes related to the subject, I have pared these down to some of the best and best known: *The Walking Dead, Shaun of the Dead, Zombieland, The Road, I Am Legend,* and *Game of Thrones,* particularly. I have consciously tried to feature works other than the seminal works of Romero, since his films have been much discussed and he has discussed them in considerable detail in interviews and documentaries. I do make reference to Romero's work where appropriate, and I'm hoping that you will leave this book with a sense of how his work has influenced the field—and how others have revised and revisited him in interesting ways. Since there is a vast and growing literature of zombie studies, I wanted to offer something new, inviting, and interesting, and I hope you will feel that this method of approaching these stories lives up to my desires for our mutual exploration.

ZOMBIE STUDIES

When there's no more room in Hell, the dead will walk the earth.
—PETER (KEN FOREE), *Dawn of the Dead*

The roots of the modern zombie are in African and Caribbean culture (the word comes from the Haitian Creole *zonbi*), and those narratives have their own powerful story to tell about race, control, and powerlessness, but our own cultural preoccupation with zombies dates to 1968 and Romero's film *Night of the Living Dead*. While previous stories and films (among them *White Zombie*, *I Walked with a Zombie*, *I Am Legend*, and *Last Man on Earth*) introduced essential elements of the zombie character and narrative, Romero's 1968 film represents the ground zero of the Zombie Apocalypse. It also marks the permanent shift away from the African/Caribbean story of zombie servants, manipulated and exploited by landowners and voodoo practitioners, and toward the narrative of ravenous walking corpses who infect others with their condition and before whom civilization itself stands in peril.[23] The central narrative of the Zombie Apocalypse introduced by Romero's films is flexible enough to accept some alterations. (In *28 Days Later*, for example, the "zombies" are living victims of the Rage, a virus; instead of the traditional shambling Romero zombies, screenwriter Alex Garland said, he came to his story via "an idea for a movie about running zombies.") But the template is clear: human characters in these stories seek to survive oncoming waves of creatures who attack and assimilate and thereby threaten the very fabric of their society.[24]

In our Ur-story, *Night of the Living Dead*, a small group of humans is trapped in a farmhouse as the walking dead prowl outside, and reports from the outer world indicate the

growing seriousness of the situation. People are being murdered left and right; some reports indicate that the murderers
are consuming their victims; and, as ever, authorities are encouraging listeners to remain calm, to remain behind closed
doors, and not to venture out. During the course of the film,
the group and we as viewers are faced with horrors. Characters
are eviscerated and eaten. A zombie child consumes its father
and kills its mother. At the movie's conclusion, the lone survivor, and the closest we have to a hero, an African American
man, is shot by a member of a sheriff's posse. In addition to
the familiar tropes of plot, this unhappy ending, as Kim
Paffenroth notes, has also become a narrative standby for
subsequent horror films, as "its hopelessness struck a chord
with people, said something meaningful to people about a
world of meaninglessness."[25] The Zombie Apocalypse, not
surprisingly, often ends badly for its characters. The two
powerful options offered in zombie narratives are hope and
nihilism, and there is little question which one audiences are
left with at the end of *Night of the Living Dead*.

Night of the Living Dead appeared in 1968 at a turbulent
time in the history of America, when an unpopular war,
changes in sexual mores and gender roles, widespread violence, and tragic assassinations filled the news. To people
living through these messy events, the world might very well
have seemed out of control, as though chaos was ascendant
and laws, regulations, and even conventional morality were
powerless to check the spread of chaos. To many people of
the time, the earlier words of the Irish poet W. B. Yeats would
have seemed eerily appropriate:

> *Things fall apart; the centre cannot hold;*
> *Mere anarchy is loosed upon the world,*
> *The blood-dimmed tide is loosed....*[26]

In many ways our own time resembles 1968, which may help explain the incredible resurgence of zombie stories following 9/11. Cultural critics note that zombie films tend to be more popular—and more numerous—in times of great uproar and upheaval, which should surprise no one; popular culture always responds to the needs of its audiences, and zombies most meaningfully walk a planet that has experienced multiple distresses.[27] Critics and scholars have noted that the zombie film is a perfect fit for a post-9/11 world, and zombie studies, reacting to the popularity of these stories, has become a booming field within the academy. The scholarly press McFarland publishes a series titled "Contributions to Zombie Studies"; scholars across the United States, United Kingdom, and elsewhere write, publish, and deliver research on the Zombie Apocalypse; and universities, including the University of California, Irvine, and the University of Baltimore, offer courses on zombies. As the *Wall Street Journal* drolly puts it, "zombies thrive on campuses" today.[28]

At their best, literary and cultural critics can help us to understand both the works that they study and our responses to them. In his seminal work of cultural criticism, for example, a survey of depression-era films titled *We're in the Money*, Andrew Bergman noted that certain Hollywood genres achieve greater popularity in times of cultural ferment. Traditional Westerns, for example, which accent the importance of law and order and affirm American society, are more popular in times that are culturally conservative, when people perceive the American experiment to be successful. When it is Morning in America, to use Ronald Reagan's phrase, Westerns and other films affirming the cultural order tend to enjoy greater currency.

Gangster films, on the other hand, which undercut the traditional American success story, and musicals, which offer straight escapism, tend to be most popular in times of economic upheaval, recession, and even depression.[29] Like gangster films, zombie stories also become more popular at times when everything seems to be falling apart, whether 1968, when *Night of the Living Dead* appeared, or 1978, when *Dawn of the Dead* appeared alongside such disturbing films as *Halloween* and *Invasion of the Body Snatchers*, or at our present moment following the 9/11 terror attacks on Washington, DC, and New York City and the 7/7 terror attacks on London.

On September 11, 2001, Americans came to an awareness of what, sadly, other people around the globe had known for some time: that there are people out there who want to kill us. *28 Days Later* appeared to popular and critical acclaim just after the 9/11 attacks, a perfect match of story and moment, and the zombie craze has not since let up. Daniel Drezner observes that "the living dead have become the hottest paranormal pop culture phenomenon of this century" and notes that well over one-third of all zombie films ever made have been released since 9/11.[30] Along with that fantastic glut of movies, we must also consider the massive success of the aforementioned post-9/11 zombie games, apps, and TV shows. Why do they appeal to us? Lenika Cruz, who participates in weekly roundtable discussions on *The Walking Dead* and *Game of Thrones* as part of her cultural coverage for the *Atlantic*, told me that zombies "tap into anxieties we have about mass destruction, biowarfare, infection, and more broadly, the vulnerability of the human body (and mind). Zombie stories tap into our fears of disease outbreaks, which in today's world have global implications. I think there's a morbid fascination with the way our bodies can betray us or be hijacked against our will—think of zombie bites as the secular version of demonic possession."[31] Max Brooks, author of *World War Z* and *The Zombie Survival Guide*, speaks from the creator's standpoint but comes to very similar conclusions: "I think [zombies] reflect our very real anxieties of these crazy scary times. A zombie story gives people a fictional lens to see the real problems of the world. You can deal with societal breakdown, famine, disease, chaos in the streets, but as long as the catalyst for all of them is zombies, you can still sleep."[32]

Popular culture and literature are often vehicles for meaning, even when their audiences consume them primarily for entertainment, and wildly popular genres and works often tap into larger concerns. This is one of the reasons for their cultural currency. In his review of Christopher Nolan's movie *The Dark Knight*, Roger Ebert observed how "these stories touch on deep fears, traumas, fantasies, and hopes," and in an article on the Hunger Games saga, John Anderson wrote in *Time*: "We bring our baggage to the movies. We always have."[33]

Cultural critic Clive Marsh affirmed this opinion in his massive empirical study of British filmgoers, through which he discovered that "philosophy, theology, and ethics are happening as furtive, incidental activities amid enjoying a supposedly escapist culture."[34] Likewise, Diane Winston notes that in the case of TV viewers, "the experience of watching, and responding to, TV characters' moral dilemmas, crises of faith, bouts of depression, and fits of exhilaration gives expression—as well as insight and resolution—to viewers' own spiritual odysseys and ethical predicaments."[35] What is true for film and TV is true across virtually every platform: whether or not we realize it, we are working out our own issues as we watch characters wrestling with the conflicts presented in their stories—or as we look at the living dead.

Rhett Reese, who wrote the Jesse Eisenberg/Woody Harrelson film *Zombieland*, told an Austin Film Festival audience that we all have fears and the zombie film is about satisfying its audience, "having them see something on screen that they feel is true inside them. Fear dominates our lives, and I think it's nice to also go to a theater and project your fear. Fear of getting fired, fear of unemployment, fear of, you know, your creepy next door neighbor, whatever it is, and project that on to something else and have it become the catch-all zombie...the thing you can then take a baseball bat and hit over the head."[36]

These are the practical musings of a professional storyteller. But note how similarly Thacker describes our modern situation: "The world is increasingly unthinkable—a world of planetary disasters, emerging pandemics, tectonic shifts, strange weather, oil-drenched seascapes, and the future, always-looming threat of extinction."[37] It is the opening of *World War Z* all over again. In comparison with that litany of disaster, a purely fantasy menace—however frightening—is indeed a comfort.

Zombies are also a reminder of the death that awaits us all—and that too, strangely, can be a comfort. One of my favorite days on the church calendar is Ash Wednesday, the entry into the Christian season of Lent. My former priest (now the Episcopal bishop of Olympia), Greg Rickel, used to encourage parishioners to take the occasion of Ash Wednesday to make a will and get their affairs in order. The liturgy, during which a cross of ashes is imposed on the forehead, is frankly depressing: "Know that you are dust, and to dust you will return." In that vision of the corpse I will become, the ashes to which I will be reduced, however, there is also peace. When I consume a zombie story, I am confronted with the visceral awareness that I will someday be a corpse (presumably not an animated one and, presumably, not because of an animated one!), and I can come to some sort of peace, whether consciously or not, with that universal truth that one day I will be rotting in a grave, or become ashes.

Valar morghulis, as we hear in *Game of Thrones. All men must die.*

As appalling as these narrative realities may be, we appreciate these stories, we find ourselves in these stories, and we are taught something by them. In these tales of the living dead, we are discovering metaphors for our own lives, answers to some of our deepest questions, and fellow travelers who convince us that we are not alone in our concerns. So these stories are entertainment—but entertainment that matters. When we sit down to watch a movie or TV show, open a book, or start a game session, we get a blast of something else in addition to entertainment.

Thus, we are drawn to these stories because they engage us on a number of levels, and popular stories of the walking dead interest us partly because of the significant material caught in their clutches. In the debut issue of the comic *The Walking Dead*, originally published in 2003, Robert Kirkman poses one simple question: How would you react if you woke up and found out that the whole world had changed? Actor Scott Reiniger, who plays Roger in Romero's *Dawn of the Dead*, says his motivation for his character was similar: "What would I do in this situation?"[38]

The back cover copy for the trade collections of *Walking Dead* comics frames the human dilemma of the Zombie Apocalypse in this way: "The world we knew is gone. The world of commerce and frivolous necessity has been replaced by a world of survival and responsibility."[39] In that world, how would you survive? In the first issue of the comic, Officer Rick Grimes wakes from a coma to discover he is alone in a deserted hospital. The only people he encounters are mindless walking corpses, and he survives his first encounter with a zombie only accidentally, breaking its neck when the two tumble down a flight of stairs as they struggle.

Outside the hospital, he encounters another of these walking dead, a female bicyclist, who lies half-eaten, crippled, and moaning in the grass. The sight shakes him: he has walked only a few feet with her bicycle when he drops to his knees weeping, and we don't know how long he is overcome with the horror. But eventually he gets to his feet and rides to his home, where he discovers that his wife and child have vanished. He meets a father and son who have moved into the house next door. They inform him that all media shut down a few weeks after "those things" began to appear, and that the walking corpses are everywhere. Rick returns to the sheriff's department, takes a squad car and some weapons, and heads out of town toward Atlanta, where he hopes he will find his wife, his son, and civilization. But before he leaves, some moral impulse impels him back to the zombie bicycle girl. He puts her out of her misery with a single shot to the head, and wipes the tears from his eyes.

He may have to do this again in a world that has been transformed almost beyond recognition.

But that doesn't mean he has to enjoy it.

Andrew Lincoln, who plays Rick in the TV series, says, "This is not a horror movie, it's a story."[40] *The Walking Dead* works within the horror genre, but as Kirkman also notes in his introduction to the first graphic novel, the horror is incidental in his mind to the big questions with which he wants to wrestle: "Good zombie movies show us how messed up we are, they make us question our station in society...and our society's station in the world....With *The Walking Dead*, I want to explore how people deal with extreme situations and how those events CHANGE them....I hope to show you reflections of your friends, your neighbors, your families, and yourselves."[41]

The Walking Dead from its beginnings as a comic book until now, then, has been a story that comments on family, society, dwindling resources, violence and the cost of violence, death, and life. It simultaneously asks "What are 'those things'?" and "What will I have to become to resist them?" Like any good story, *The Walking Dead* carries layers of meaning, though, and it offers us a number of characters whose actions can be parsed for life wisdom. Rick, for example, begins as a sort of Gary Cooper character who, very much against his will, becomes the leader of a group fighting to survive in that world where everything has changed. He stands in for all of us. In combating zombies and bandits and seeking to survive, he represents our own battles against all that stands in our way in life (presumably not zombies in our case) and our own struggles between living courageously and asking the very human question "How much longer do I have to do this?"

This last is a question that gets at *why* we live—why we struggle, why, in Hamlet's words, we continue to bear "the whips and scorns of time, / The oppressor's wrong, the proud man's contumely," what exactly it is that makes us human—questions I'll explore in chapter 1 with the help of zombie narratives.[42] (Rick, like many characters confronting the Zombie Apocalypse, also allows us other reflections on ourselves, but considering that he is our entry character into this bewildering world of the Zombie Apocalypse, this seems the

important question with which to open. What is the difference between the living and the living dead?)

Michonne (portrayed on the show by Danai Gurira) illuminates another central concern explored in zombie stories. When we first meet her on *The Walking Dead*, she is a
solitary warrior, a zombie-slaying hard case bearing a samu-
rai's katana and yanking along two zombies in chains—later
revealed to be her boyfriend and his best friend. Kirkman
said that Gurira was cast because she captured the character's strength and intensity and at the same time exhibited
Michonne's emotional vulnerability, her need for community.[43] When Michonne encounters the other survivors, it
launches a central set of questions about *with whom* we live:
"Can I become part of a community? Why would I want to?"
Her choice as an outsider to become a part of Rick's ragtag
band offers us lessons in the human need for community and
all the gifts and terrors that come along with that need. As
she enters into a relationship with Rick in deeper and deeper
ways, she also teaches us something about how we need each
other. I'll consider the lessons of the Zombie Apocalypse
about community in chapter 2.

The journey of Daryl (played by Norman Reedus on the
show; he has no analog in the comics) offers us another
lesson, one with power for many of us. He is a leather-clad
biker who is too comfortable with violence—our first encounter with him is stunning in its intensity and frightening
in how his every movement seems to be to hurt, kill, or in-
timidate—yet the back of his leather jacket bears angels'
wings. As Reedus himself says, those wings have "really
become a symbol for Daryl's arc.... You see the front and he
looks like a dirty biker dude, then you see the back and there's
heart there. He doesn't want you to see that softer side of

him, but on the back there's that little hint of hope that this guy's not as bad as you think he is."[44] With Daryl and other characters in *The Walking Dead*, we are asking a third important question explored in the zombie narrative: "Can I be a better person? And what would it mean to be a better person?" These are questions about ethics, questions about *how* we live and how we *ought* to live, and, as you might now expect, chapter 3 is devoted to the lessons of zombie narratives on this topic as well.

Maggie (Lauren Cohan) offers us a final example of how zombie narratives can help us wrestle with existential human questions. Everyone in the world of *The Walking Dead* has suffered, of course; early on in the comic Andrea recites a litany of those she has lost: "My friends, my family, my neighbors, my co-workers...everyone. Everyone in this group is dealing with that."[45] In season 5 of the TV show Maggie experiences a run of losses (her father, her sister, her farm) that could be paralyzing. In the face of such disaster piled on disaster, how will she respond? She asks herself: "Is there any way I can survive these losses? Is there hope somewhere in this, or should I give up?" Is life meaningless and the world headed only toward death and destruction (a nihilistic view we find in zombie narratives like *Night of the Living Dead* and *Dawn of the Dead*, among others) or can some good emerge from this disaster? (This is a common theme in apocalyptic literature and was the hope of J. R. R. Tolkien, who coined the word "eucatastrophe" to describe just such an outcome.) This is a question about *where* our lives are going, whether there is meaning in the cosmos; chapter 4 explores what stories of the apocalypse (and particularly the Zombie Apocalypse) have to say on this topic.

The zombies of *The Walking Dead* and other narratives are rarely differentiated characters, but they carry a heavy freight of meaning. On one level, of course, they can be stock horror villains, groaning toward us with clutching hands outstretched. But, echoing Max Brooks, Raina Kelley notes in *Newsweek* that these zombies represent a lot more: "At a time when the average person doesn't know what to fear most—terrorism, global warming, pandemics like cholera, economic collapse, random gun violence, rogue nuclear weapons—zombies are the monster du jour, encompassing all those things."[46] Zombies are multivalent. They can be whatever we require them to be, whatever keeps us awake at night. Perhaps it is true, as Stephen Marche notes in *Esquire*, that zombie movies help us confront our fears but "don't give us a particularly helpful plan for dealing with them," beyond the illusion of agency in the face of oncoming perils. But that, as he notes, is still something.[47] At the close of any zombie story, we can close the comic, shut the book, turn off the TV or computer, and return to our lives a little reassured that whatever our own personal demons might be, they are not so bad as this.

And for better or worse, the world keeps on turning.

In his survey of how human beings have understood life after death, *After Lives: A Guide to Heaven, Hell, and Purgatory*, John Casey argues that our intellectual attempts to explain what comes next "derive from fear of extinction" or "from a hope that a future world might compensate for the evils of this one."[48] So too do our stories of the walking dead. The fear is self-evident. For millennia, humans seem to have been concerned with keeping the dead in their proper place, a place that is not anywhere near us, and one of the central frissons of zombie tales is the dread of contact. But these stories also suggest that whatever happens to us at death, that daunting boundary may not mark the end. Some piece of us may survive. Of course, these stories suggest that life after death will be a sort of nonexperiencing existence, that we will not know our loved ones, or that even in death we will not be able to control our basest instincts to consume. On the other hand some zombie stories suggest that the life to come may not differ much from our lives now.

Because these stories take place in this strange borderland between death and life, they may also offer us the wisdom to begin changing our lives now. In Romero's *Dawn of the Dead*, for example, zombies and humans alike congregate at the shopping mall, a commentary on the fact that sometimes, as film critic Moira Macdonald observes, we are already sunk in "the kind of life that can turn a man into the walking dead."[49] Such a thought should give us pause. So too should the argument of Calder-Williams that maybe one of the things that scares us about zombies is not merely that we may in some way be like them but that we will be like them forever, that zombies may represent not just frightening change but a horrid and unchanging status quo.[50] Are we doomed to consume forever without enjoyment or awareness? Can we break free of this cycle of unliving?

Zombies can also represent the fear of losing one's identity, of being assimilated. Early in the writing of this book, I had a familiar nightmare in which Things were coming for me—they looked human (the one looking out the window next door was wearing the Roman collar of a priest) but wanted to turn me into something like themselves. If I became one of them, I would no longer be myself, not as I understand myself. And, of course, in this dream my front door refused to lock, so there was little hope that I could keep them out—unless I woke up. This narrative of creeping assimilation is not just familiar to us from horror stories but is a common topic of science fiction as well: *Invasion of the Body Snatchers, The Thing, The Stepford Wives, The World's End*, and episodes of *Doctor Who, Supernatural,* and *X-Files* all center on this fear. In these stories, we are left to defend ourselves against waves of creatures who want to steal our autonomy, our awareness, and our very selves.

Taken together, these stories are not simply reflections of our free-floating anxieties about current events. They also express some of our most deep-seated fears: the fear of non-existence; the fear of being helpless; the fear of being forced to change; the fear of being unable to change. So, yes, zombie stories are about AIDS and terrorism and Ebola and economic unrest. But they are also about existential human questions—and some of our provisional attempts to answer them. Thus, as we examine the ways that literature and popular entertainment have raised the dead and set them walking, we venture into the intellectual disciplines of theology, politics, psychology, economics, narratology, and philosophy. We will recognize how culture and history shape and are reflected by the entertainment we consume. But I hope that this journey will also show us how these books, movies, games, and other entertainments have been shaping us.

Human beings have been watching and hearing about the walking dead for centuries. By entering now into these contemporary stories with consciousness and intention, we might learn things that affect the way we walk through our lives from this day forward. If we can do that, then whether or not we ever watch another zombie film, living with the living dead will have achieved good ends.

LIFE, DEATH, AND ZOMBIES

Who Are the Living Dead?

Nothing is more certain than death, and nothing uncertain but its hour.

—ENGUERRAND DE COUCY (1397)

I have seen the dead walk.

—THE LORD COMMANDER OF THE NIGHT'S WATCH, IN GEORGE R. R. MARTIN, *A Clash of Kings: A Song of Ice and Fire*

A CULTURAL HISTORY OF THE LIVING DEAD

A MATH BLOG FOR *SCIENTIFIC AMERICAN* recently reported that a mathematician, Sarah Reehl, ran a study on the rise of the zombie phenomenon using models similar to those employed for the spread of infectious diseases. Her conclusions: "Zombie fever will peak around the year 2038," although interest will not return to pre-9/11 numbers for another fifty-plus years.[1] If we needed scientific evidence beyond the sheer quantity and popularity of zombie stories, comic events, and products I've already noted, here it is: zombies have taken over the world and have no intention of relinquishing it any time soon.

Not everyone understands why and how zombies have accomplished this. After all, they're slow, they can't plan, they lack group cohesion. They're not capable of change. They're not, frankly, capable of a lot of things we like to see from engaging characters. As Manuel Gonzales puts it in "Escape from the Mall," his masterful fictional deconstruction of the zombie genre, "truth be told, zombie-like creatures aren't known for their ability to speak.

"Nor for their understanding of ironic timing.

"Or even their understanding of delayed gratification."[2]

Because of these limitations, some people find zombie stories uninteresting and zombies themselves uninteresting. *New Yorker* critic Sarah Larson, despite her love for *Game of Thrones*, finds the wights the least-interesting aspect of the show, saying that they carry "the emotional pull of an army of ants, minus the ants' dignified social structures and attractive formic-acid exoskeletons," and she is hardly alone in her opinion.[3] In addition to the fascination I have often encountered over the past two years when I told people I was writing about the Zombie Apocalypse, I have also sometimes been met with bewilderment.

My friend Sarah Bird, an acclaimed novelist and screenwriter, recently confessed to me over pints at a North Campus pub in our hometown of Austin, Texas, "Greg, I don't get it. I want to. I see zombies everywhere. But the whole thing seems so bizarre to me."

I understood her. Despite my passion for this book and its topic, I would not describe myself as a zombie fanatic. The living dead also seem, at first, a strange entertainment choice to me. Like many people over the age of eighteen, I no longer take much delight in being frightened, or in consuming gore for gore's sake. I sometimes feel, in fact, more disturbed than enlightened by these stories of the walking dead. But as a writer, cultural critic, and theologian, it has seemed to me that something important is going on that I need to understand

and help others understand; like my friend, I see zombies everywhere, and I want to know why.

On that afternoon in Austin, I looked across the table at Sarah and summed up what I had discovered in two years of research on two continents: "When humanity seems to be facing an extinction-level event, the dead get up and walk around."

I explained that this may happen in art, it may happen in stories, it may, as today, happen in movies, TV, and gaming, but for centuries human artists and writers have employed contact with and depiction of death as a tool in times of turmoil. Sometimes it's an awareness of mortality expressed in the exhibition of corpses; sometimes it's a personified Living Death interacting with the living. Although our normal lives in 2016 work hard to keep Death well away from us—we typically do our dying among medical professionals and let funerary professionals put us cleanly and beautifully away—Death has a way of slipping free, percolating to the surface, rising in front of us so we cannot ignore him. Whether we speak of the plague years of the Middle Ages, the trenches of World War I, the Holocaust, or the post-9/11 years, we should not be surprised to be confronted by the walking dead in imaginative works. It seems to be a natural human defense mechanism in difficult times.

John Casey writes that the earliest funerary practices indicate attempts to propitiate the dead to keep them where they are. Early humans did not want the dead crossing back across the boundaries any more than we do. He notes that as we examine some of the earliest burial practices, they seem to be based on "fear, and fear not of one's own death, but of the dead... dread of the terrifyingly capricious things the dead are deemed capable of inflicting upon the living."[4] At some point in human development, though, humans seem to have lived into the awareness that all of us are going to wind up wherever it is the dead are. As cultures develop stories about where the dead go, and it becomes obvious that everyone on the planet will someday join them, funerary practices begin to accommodate these understandings. They become less about keeping the dead in their place and more, perhaps, about the awareness that death has a place among us.

Recently in a churchyard in Wales I stopped to examine a gravestone. Its inscription was eroded, and the surface of the stone covered with moss, but I could still tease out the words, which proved to be similar to many inscriptions nearby, and to many others I have read over the years:

> *In Memory of John Jones of Shotton*
> *who died*
> *Feb 9th 1845*
> *Aged 24 Years*
>
> *Weep not my wife and children dear*
> *A tender father lieth here*
> *My death you know my grave you see*
> *Prepare yourself to follow me.*

Death walks back into the lives of the living as the awareness that someday, now or later, we are all going to follow John Jones of Shotton. *Valar morghulis*, as *Game of Thrones* reminds us: All men must die. Sometimes, perhaps, we need to be reminded of the coming of death. The point of this particular inscription is that without such a reminder, its readers might not be facing the reality of death as squarely as they ought and living accordingly. At other times, however, death is more obvious, and we seem to encounter it everywhere we look.

The Middle Ages were a time when Death could not be kept segregated from the living. Popular historian William Manchester describes the way "the Dark Ages were stark in every dimension. Famines and plagues, culminating in the Black Death and its recurring pandemics, repeatedly thinned the population." In addition to disease, he notes, the Middle Ages witnessed climatic changes, political unrest, pervasive violence, religious and cultural turmoil, and indeed a multitude of ills that look remarkably familiar to us today.[5] Not only could death not be sequestered, it spilled over into everyday life. Not surprisingly, perhaps, medieval art and literature often depicted corpses and even personified Death. Instead of hiding death away—impossible at the time— people in the Middle Ages often confronted death through their religious practices and their culture, as well as in their daily lives.

Writers and artists of the Middle Ages employed two major types of references to Death, the memento mori, and the Dance of the Dead. Memento mori (Latin: "Remember that you must die") are reminders of the fleeting nature of life and the inescapable nature of death. Like the gravestone in Wales, memento mori encourage those who look, read, or listen to accept that life is fleeting and death inevitable. This realization should prompt some decisions about how to live life in preparation for that death. Often these are pious and religious decisions, but at the very least, memento mori might encourage a heightened awareness of life and the pursuit of a good life, however that might be understood.

Gravestones and funerary monuments very often present examples of memento mori. The monument of Edward the

Black Prince at Canterbury Cathedral proffers the motto "Such as you are, so once was I / As I am now, so shalt thou be." One popular manifestation of the memento mori was the *transi*, or cadaver tomb, a monument that included a representation of a corpse—often eaten by worms—or a skeleton, in addition to or even in place of a representation of the way the deceased had appeared in life. Across the choir from the Black Prince at Canterbury is the tomb of the fifteenth-century archbishop of Canterbury Henry Chichele, which graphically displays the contrast at the heart of the transi: while the elaborate and colorful upper part of the tomb shows the archbishop in garb befitting his lordly station, the lower part of the tomb depicts his naked and emaciated corpse. The inscription on Chichele's tomb reads "I was pauper-born, then to primate raised. Now I am cut down and served up for worms. Behold my grave."

A similar sort of awareness about death emerges in the Danse Macabre, or Dance of the Dead (Totentanz in German). In stories and images, the living people of every station, from emperor to pope to merchant and peasant, are confronted by Death, literally and figuratively. Art historian Johan Huizinga has described the motif, in beautifully paradoxical terms, as "the most popular description of decay known to the Middle Ages."[6] Perhaps the best-known artistic depiction of the Danse Macabre was a fifteenth-century painting in the Hall of Columns at the Cemetery of the Innocents in Paris. A fifteenth-century bronze sculpture of Death stood in the Hall of Columns, surrounded by the Danse Macabre fresco and heaps of real human bones. Although the fresco and the cemetery no longer exist, today you may see this version of Death in the Louvre, and it remains a startling figure even divorced from its context. His arm raised in threat or warning, this figure very much resembles the menacing zombies we have come to know and (some of us) love.

In these and many other images, sculptures, poems, sermons, and stories of the Middle Ages, death permeates the culture; imagine these as somehow equivalent to a few of those hundreds of thousands of zombie items we mentioned for sale on Amazon. But the Middle Ages was hardly the only period in human history when people were coming face-to-face with death on a daily basis and the dead began to walk in their cultural forms as well. Historian Barbara Tuchman has explicitly made connections between the plague years of the Middle Ages and the trench warfare of World War I. In both cases, she describes the pessimism engendered when a terrible event does not bring about a better world. The two periods also contain other similarities in situation and in their representation of death and suffering.[7]

The Dance of the Dead, a series of etchings by British soldier Percy Delf Smith (originals at the Imperial War Museum in London), takes the tradition he inherited from the Middle Ages but updates the images for his own time's crisis. In Smith's works, the figure of Death accompanies soldiers into battle, sits brooding over the blasted battlefield, and in one notable etching, "Death Awed," stands amazed and gazes at two boots, which, with their protruding fragments of bone and foot, are all that remain of some soldier obliterated moments ago by artillery. Smith's point was and remains powerful: even Death stops and marvels at the destructive powers of human beings, laid bare for the world to see in trench warfare.

Other artists of the period also made a connection between medieval art and their horrific present. A German medallion sculpted by Ludwig Gies in the collection of the British

Museum bears the inscription "Totentanz, 1914–1917," and shows a skeletal Death leading a group of German soldiers off to a battle where they will almost certainly perish. Another German version of the Dance of Death, Otto Wirsching's "Vom Totentanz" (1915), clearly draws from medieval woodcuts and the work of earlier artists like Hans Holbein while updating the images to include modern warfare and familiar but modern characters who are visited and seized by Death: the Officer, the Thief, the Beggar, the Jew, the Nun, the Orphan.

In addition to the revived Danse Macabre, many landscape paintings and photos made during World War I reinforce the common theme of Death omnipresent. Imperial War Museum curator Alexandra Walton drew my attention to the work of the prominent British artist Paul Nash, who painted blasted battlefield after blasted battlefield, the blackened and beaten trees standing as mute witnesses to death and destruction. "The trees are people," Walton explained to me. Paul Gough notes that "Nash saw all this. In the Ypres Salient he was aghast at the sight of splintered copses and dismembered trees, seeing in their shattered limbs an equivalent for the human carnage that lay all around or even hung in shreds from the eviscerated treetops. In so many of his war pictures, the trees remain inert and gaunt, failing to respond to the shafts of sunlight; their branches dangle lifelessly."[8] Even though no human corpses are visible, it's a landscape of death.

It's not only through the visual arts that this blasted landscape enters into the zeitgeist. Numerous writers described no-man's-land and the desolation that comes with death and battle. The American nurse Mary Borden wrote about the devastation at the Somme and the experience of each individual soldier, alone although surrounded by thousands, in what feels like a landscape of death personified:

With the earth shaking—
With the solid earth under his feet giving way—
With the hills covered with fire and the valleys smoking,
    and the few bare trees spitting bullets....
With the few houses broken, no walls, no enclosure, no
    protection.
With all the universe crashing upon him, rain, sun, cold,
    dark, death, coming full on him.[9]

Nor did one have to witness the trenches firsthand to realize how the world had changed, the expanded menace to the species. T. S. Eliot's poem *The Waste Land* has been presented to generations of bored students as a literary masterpiece, which it is; and it is a poem of genuine power and menace. Before Ezra Pound advised Eliot to remove it, *The Waste Land* bore an epigraph from Joseph Conrad's *Heart of Darkness*, one of the most nihilistic of modernist texts; the poem encapsulates many of the themes of Eliot's post–World War I work: ennui, desperation, bleak futility, blasted yet tenuous hope. Early in the poem, the poet asks:

What are the roots that clutch, what branches grow
Out of this stony rubbish? Son of man,
You cannot say, or guess, for you know only
A heap of broken images, where the sun beats,
And the dead tree gives no shelter, the cricket no relief,
And the dry stone no sound of water.[10]

As we visit the paintings of Nash and other World War I artists, it seems we are reentering a familiar and frightening disturbing world in which nothing lives—and perhaps nothing can live.

Some of America's best-known postwar writers also drew on this imagery of the blasted landscape. Ernest Hemingway's short story "Big Two-Hearted River" follows a returning World War I veteran, Hemingway surrogate Nick Adams, whose internal brokenness is mirrored by the external countryside, which is nothing but the "burnt timber" he first encounters: "There was no town, nothing but the rails and the burned-over country.... The stone was chipped and split by the fire. It was all that was left of the town of Seney. Even the surface had been burned off the ground."[11] A better-known evocation of this wasted landscape is found in F. Scott Fitzgerald's novel *The Great Gatsby*. On an ancient billboard for an eye doctor, giant eyes look out over a blasted plain: "A valley of ashes—a fantastic farm where ashes grow like wheat into ridges and hills and grotesque gardens; where ashes take the forms of houses and chimneys and rising smoke and, finally, with a transcendent effort, of ash-grey men, who move dimly and already crumbling through the powdery air."[12] In these word-pictures, one can flash forward to the valley of ashes described at the beginning of Cormac McCarthy's novel *The Road*; this is the landscape of apocalypse.

Faced with the horrors of the trenches and the dead landscape, the living too can become walking dead, a reality captured by Wilfred Owen. In "Insensibility," he writes that it is easier to become dead than live through the death all around:

Happy are men who yet before they are killed
Can let their veins run cold....
And some cease feeling
Even themselves or for themselves.
Dullness best solves the tease and doubt of shelling.[13]

Other poets of the period also captured the triumph and presence of death: the Scottish soldier Charles Sorley, who died in action in 1915, perhaps evokes our images of the Zombie Apocalypse more strongly than any other World War I–era writer in a poem discovered after his death from a sniper's bullet:

> *When you see millions of the mouthless dead*
> *Across your dreams in pale battalions go....*
> *Give them not praise. For, deaf, how should they know*
> *It is not curses heaped on each gashed head?*
> *Nor tears. Their blind eyes see not your tears flow.*
> *Nor honour. It is easy to be dead.*[14]

In times of potential extinction, artists and storytellers have clearly seen that confrontations with Death serve a valuable function. We encounter a landscape of Death—or images of the walking dead—in art and photography from the Holocaust, for example. The American photographer Margaret Bourke-White's iconic 1945 "The Living Dead at Buchenwald" bears a haunting likeness to modern fictional scenes of the living dead. British artist Dorothy Zinkeisen, who arrived at Bergen-Belsen just after that camp was liberated, spoke of the "simply ghastly sight of skeleton bodies just flung out of the huts" and painted what she saw.[15] We likewise find living skeletons and embodied Death in art produced by survivors of the atomic bombings of Hiroshima and Nagasaki, by artists on both sides of the Vietnam conflict, and today, in art growing out of genocides and terror attacks around the globe. Which brings us back to 1968 and *The Night of the Living Dead*, and all the way forward to the present, when Death walks most prominently in our culture in the form of zombies.

All of these eras have felt to those who lived in them like moments of high human drama and distress, and, not surprisingly, the dead got up and presented themselves to view in much the same way the dead shamble across the landscape in our own heated moment. While the art and narratives from these times may not function as entertainment in the way our zombie stories do, they do, perhaps, have some of the same meaning-making value. In a world where we may feel menaced by equally terrifying threats, it should not surprise us that, as in times past, Death walks in our art, literature, and entertainment.

But to return to the question posed by my writer friend: Why zombies?

Part of the answer can be found in the ways that zombies resemble us yet differ from us. They are near enough to being human to offer comparison and different enough to offer contrast. In the course of those comparisons, we begin to discover what we believe life is, what death is, and how in the strange gray areas that lie between, we must make important choices about what it means to live.

THE LIVING, THE DEAD, AND THE LIVING DEAD

What I was, once, alive, I still am, dead.

— DANTE, *The Inferno*, canto 14, line 51

When I was a hospital chaplain in the mid-2000s, I found myself in close proximity to the dying and the dead in ways I have not been, thankfully, before or since. Like many Westerners, I knew little about death firsthand. I had never seen anything larger than a bird or small animal die; I had never touched a corpse. So during my first on-call weekend, although I knew the experience was coming, I was more than a little nervous when I was called into the Seton Hospital Emergency Room, where a patient was expiring on the table while doctors and nurses worked on him furiously. He was motionless beneath their ministrations, some of which were violent. I couldn't help but stare—which may have tipped off the care team that I was the one useless person in the room.

"You need to go out to the family," one of the nurses said, pulling me aside, "and get them ready. He's probably not going to make it."

"Right," I told her. "Sure thing." I nodded to her with much more assurance than I felt. I stepped to the entrance of the ER, took a deep breath, and stepped out into the waiting room.

Five faces looked up at me. Keeping my face neutral, I stepped across the room to them, introduced myself as the chaplain, and began to prepare them for the worst. I couldn't, of course, tell them that the patient was going to die. That is a medical judgment, and I am not a medical doctor. I was never even allowed to tell someone their loved one was dead. How would I really know? But I did have a vocabulary for the transition that I was told was taking place, taught me by seminary friends who had previously done their chaplaincies. People had to be eased into thinking of their loved one—alive when last they saw them—as moving from that state to death.

"The doctors are working on him now," I told them. "But you need to know this. Right now, he is the sickest person in this hospital."

The wife looked up at me, weeping, but the sister-in-law nodded. She could take in that news.

Some twenty minutes later, an ER doctor came in to notify the family that they had done all they could. Their loved one was dead. If they wanted to see the body, it would be a few minutes before they moved it.

They did want to see the body. And they asked me to go with them and lead them in prayer. So, for the first time in my life, I walked into a room where a person lay dead. Under that sheet lay a dead man. A few minutes before, he had been alive, a creature like me. Now he was motionless, thoughtless, senseless.

In zombie movies, it's right about this moment that the figure under the sheet sits up and tries to eat everyone within arm's length. If I'd thought about that very hard, I might have slipped silently out of the room, but fortunately, there was no time to think, only to act. The family formed a ring around the bed and they asked me to pray. I dropped my hand onto the man's shoulder—his cold, dead shoulder, a part of me could not help thinking—and then I began to offer what I hoped were words of comfort.

Because I was concentrating on my job, on the family, I could ignore the hard, heavy lump of lifeless flesh beneath my hand. But I remained conscious then—and became so every time I saw a dead body that summer—that some strange and powerful action had taken place that separated me from the human shape I was touching. Was it only that I was upright and conscious? Was it that I was sensible of the difference between us? What exactly *was* the difference between us? How could I learn something important about life from these encounters with death?

In *Shaun of the Dead*, we follow the story of Shaun (Simon Pegg) and his best mate, Ed (Nick Frost), working-class guys who stumble through their days like, well, zombies.

That the living and the undead might bear startling similarities is not a new insight from a horror film (in *Dawn of the Dead*, Romero drew similar parallels between ghouls meandering through the Monroeville shopping mall and humans gleefully plucking products from department store shelves), but it's rarely presented with such directness and wit. Throughout the film, viewers of *Shaun of the Dead* are asked to consider just how closely characters—and they themselves—may be related to the unthinking, unliving undead. The theme of the movie is encapsulated by a "to do" list Shaun has written on his kitchen whiteboard:

> **Go round mums**
> **Get Liz back**
> **Sort Life out!**

Clearly the title of the film is more than just a clever play on *Dawn of the Dead*; it's also a reference to the emotional and spiritual state in which we find Shaun at the opening of the story. This Shaun of the dead must learn to live during the course of the story, but the challenge he faces is hardly his alone. It's a central problem in Western culture. In the movie's trailer, a voiceover asks, "Do you ever think modern life is not for you? Do you do the same dead-end job every day?...Is your love life dying on its feet?...Have you ever felt you're turning into a zombie?" The movie also asks this question from its opening moments. As they sit together—yet again—in the Winchester, a pub, Shaun's girlfriend Liz (Kate Ashfield) tells Shaun that their life together is deadening: "I want to live a little. I want you to want to do it too." For Liz, sitting at the pub every night with Shaun, Ed, and her flatmates has become worse than routine. It is sucking the life from her.

Liz is far from the only one lost in a sort of living death. Over the opening credits, the camera slowly tracks right to reveal workers stuck in mechanical repetition (including Mary, the checkout girl who will shortly appear, zombified, in Shaun's backyard), commuters checking their phones in synchronized unison, youth with headphones on shambling aimlessly down an alley, heads bobbing together. Shaun himself lurches across his bedroom after rising from slumber, lets out an inarticulate groan, then ambles downstairs and mechanically takes up a game controller—before Ed reminds him that he has work. He rides a bus, surrounded by slack-jawed and unfocused commuters. At his job at an electronics store, he struggles to motivate a workforce made up of slouching teens, then stands motionless and expressionless switching through TV channels for customers, even as the news of the first horrible stages of the zombie outbreak begins to unfold unnoticed on the screens behind him.

"I know you don't want to be here forever," Shaun tells one of his slacker employees about the existence they share. "I've got things I want to do with my life."

"When?" comes the boy's incredulous response.

When indeed? One of the most tangible themes explored in *Shaun of the Dead* is how easily people can find themselves caught in a state that is not really life. The simple fact that Shaun and Ed are converting oxygen to carbon dioxide, that their bodies are in motion, does not mean that they are truly alive. Too often we are content to act out what Henry David Thoreau called lives of quiet desperation, lives lived for such unworthy things that it is as if we are not living at all. In *Walden*, Thoreau encapsulated the reason for his experiment at Walden Pond: "I went to the woods because I wished to live deliberately, to front only the essential facts of life, and see if I could not learn what it had to teach, and not, when I came to die, discover that I had not lived. I did not wish to live what was not life, living is so dear; nor did I wish to practise resignation, unless it was quite necessary."[16]

For Thoreau, as for other thinkers before and since, human beings too often settle for pale semblances of life. They live tiny lives—lives of quiet desperation—when they are called to live large. The second-century Christian thinker Irenaeus argued that "the glory of God is the human person fully alive."[17] Gautama Buddha said: "If there is anything to be done, do it well; do it firmly and energetically." (Sometimes this is translated: "If anything is worth doing, do it with all your heart.")[18] Life is about more than moving through your days unaware; it is about being present, about choosing well, about living large.

Zombie stories often explore the question of what it means to be human by showing us the transition from one state to the other, a movement so shocking that we often stand, like Shaun and Ed, mouths wide open, simultaneously marveling and horrified at the changes taking place. Toward the end of *Night of the Living Dead*, the dying Harry (Karl Hardman) stumbles into the cellar, where his daughter, Karen (Kyra Schon), lies dead. A few moments later, when Harry's wife, Helen (Marilyn Eastman), enters Karen is no longer an inanimate body—or their little girl. In one of the most justly famed scenes from the film, Helen finds Karen eating her father. Shortly afterward, Karen also murders the stunned Helen. What happened in the interim? How did this little girl go from Karen to corpse to walking dead? Screenwriter Mark Protosevich spoke about the first time he saw the film as a child—in a theater full of other children: "Every kid in that theater went silent and still. That was probably the first time

I ever felt genuine terror in a movie theater. The idea that someone you love could want to eat you was genuinely terrifying. That you could know someone and love someone and that everything that you loved about them is gone."[19]

As zombie narratives record the transition between these stages, they offer us some of the opportunity for reflection that I had in my hospital chaplaincy. In a short span of time, something can move from one state to another—and in zombie tales, to something else again.

In *Dawn of the Dead*, Peter watches as Roger, who has been bitten and has asked his friend to "take care of me when I go," since "I don't want to be walking around like that," makes his transition. He fades, visibly weaker and sicker. He lies motionless. And then—as in my nightmare vision in the hospital—his body sits up. At the end of "Hardhome" in *Game of Thrones*, the camera pans slowly across the bodies of the human dead, Wildlings and members of the Night's Watch killed in battle with wights and the Others. As we watch, their bodies jerk, their eyes flick open, lit by a ghastly blue light, and they clamber slowly upright. And in *Shaun of the Dead*, the transformation of Shaun's stepfather, Philip (Bill Nighy), into a zombie in the back seat of his beloved Jaguar causes a lively, horrific, and finally, quite funny few moments. Shaun, his mum, and his friends scramble to get out of the car, Philip tries to detain and eat them, and heavy metal music blares from the car's speakers.

After they escape and have locked zombie Philip in the car, Shaun tries to tell his mum: "That's not even your husband in there. Okay. I know it looks like him, but there is nothing of the man you loved in that car, nothing." (Well, something, perhaps; in common with his former self, zombie Philip apparently still can't abide heavy metal and somehow manages to turn off the stereo.) But the point, for Shaun, is in the stark contrast. Seconds before he died, Philip was confessing to Shaun, perhaps even apologizing for all the years he had been so strict with him as a parent. "I always loved you, Shaun. And I always thought you had it in you to do well.... You just needed motivation, someone you could look up to, and I thought it could be me." Compare that tough love with zombie Philip's bared fangs, thrashing hands, and implicit promise of destruction to anyone he gets those hands on and you see why Shaun can tell his mother that nothing of his stepfather remains in the car.

Zombie stories do offer us meaningful examples of how to differentiate between them and us. Humans are capable of love and sacrifice; zombies are not. Humans can plan; zombies cannot. Humans can choose not to consume and destroy; zombies have no such choice. We find some notable exceptions, of course. The sentient Marvel zombies find their morality overwhelmed by their hunger, but this does not mean that they necessarily feel good about the choices they make; the zombie Peter Parker/Spiderman constantly regrets eating his Aunt May and his wife, Mary Jane. In *iZombie*, Olivia "Liv" Moore's (Rose McIver) zombie hunger forces her to eat brains, but she at least tries to limit her consumption to those of the already dead. The zombie narrator in Manuel Gonzales's short story "All of Me" fights daily with the compunctions of "the zombie in me" to bite his receptionist, Barbara, to break the neck of his boss, Keith, or to eat the face of Barbara's husband, Mark. The narrator avoids the elevator because it is "a dangerous place for someone like me. It is a place full of urges, of somewhat violent urges. There is this urge, for instance.

"Well. On second thought, no.

"In fact, I'd rather not go into detail. Let's leave it at this: It is a place for urges, which is why I take the stairs."[20]

If we have noted negative comparisons—that human beings too often are barely living the lives they've been given—nonetheless, the narrative of the Zombie Apocalypse suggests other understandings of what it means that humans live, and that they want to go on living in the face of almost certain death and destruction. Something about the characters in these films—and about us, the readers, viewers, or players of these stories—seeks to be a human person fully alive, to do whatever is worth doing with all our hearts. Zombies seem to be driven by strange urges that are shadows to our own; in the acting out of these urges and impulses, they seem to resemble us, but in their motives, of course, they cannot. Except in these rare stories in which zombies have consciousness, even souls, they are pure creatures of the physical. While the zombie hero (Billy Connolly) of the satirical film *Fido* ends up taking over a house and a wife, he is the lone emancipated zombie in the story; the others, for good reason, remain tamed by shock collars, staggering along, as Manohla Dargis writes in her *New York Times* review, "like stunned toddlers."[21] Zombies eat because they hunger; they have no higher motivation.

That often renders the difference between us starkly. In *The Walking Dead*, Rick enters Atlanta on his horse and is mobbed by zombies who tear the animal to pieces. He goes from dread to anger and indignation that these things with human forms—this early in the story, there is much Rick still does not know about zombies—could do such a thing. In the comic, Rick screams "Bastards! What the hell is wrong with you?"[22] What is wrong, of course, is that although these creatures bear the semblance of humanity, they no longer possess agency.

In stories modeled on George Romero zombies, the undead are merely physical remnants of the living: skeletons walking, zombies lurching, ghouls directed only by this hunger for flesh. Death is a boundary that alters all who cross it. Angela Kang has said, "When you're dead, what is the thing that leaves? The soul, if there is one."[23] In these stories, zombies may indeed retain some of the visible aspects of the living. But they are generally bodies vacated by souls, and they are certainly no longer the persons they once were, and this is reflected in our stories as well. Max Brooks writes in *The Zombie Survival Guide* that when someone becomes a zombie, "no matter who a person was in his former life, that person is gone, replaced by a mindless automaton with no instinct other than for feeding."[24]

You can't be too careful. Perhaps that is why Edd interrogates the resurrected Jon Snow in season 6 of *Game of Thrones*, looking him over closely and making certain his eyes don't bear the ghastly blue of the raised wights: "Your eyes are still brown. Are you still you in there?"

Jon replies, "I think so. Hold off on burning my body for now."

"That's funny," Edd says to the famously doleful Jon. "You sure that's still you in there?"

Well, he should ask these things. Death normally changes everything, and once the soul departs, that which is essentially human normally departs with it. It is a boundary that cannot be crossed, and the soul and body cannot normally be rejoined. It is in what constitutes our humanity—our soul, if there is one—that we find the most obvious ways to differentiate ourselves from these lifelike but unliving monsters.

Sometimes we equate our humanity with our ability to persevere, even when circumstances pile up against us. The end of the movie *Die Hard* offers a notable version of this archetypal story. John McLane (Bruce Willis) has been in combat with a skyscraper full of terrorists; he has watched people die and been unable to save them; he has been blown up, he has fallen down an airshaft, he has been knocked off the building and set on fire; his feet are bleeding from crossing a floor covered with broken glass. Like a survivor in a zombie story, he has endured the unthinkable, and all but unbearable stress can be read from his wounds, his rags, and the grime and sweat with which he is marked. In the final confrontation with the group's maniacal leader, Hans Gruber (Alan Rickman), who has kidnapped McLane's wife (Bonnie Bedelia), we see McLane limp into the light, battered and bruised but unbeaten. As long as there is life, this scene suggests, there is hope. The human spirit will prevail.

In the short story "Escape from the Mall," Manuel Gonzales retells an archetypal scene in the midst of the Zombie Apocalypse. A young boy named Tyrone has just watched his father charge into a mob of zombies with a baseball bat to allow him to escape, and the narrator records how the leader of the survivors, Roger, engages Tyrone afterward:

> Roger sat on his haunches and held Tyrone by the shoulders and looked deep into his eyes and told him, "That makes you the man of the house, now, Tyrone."
>
> Told him, "Do you think you're ready for that?"
>
> And then when Tyrone shook his head no, and while the rest of us, I'm sure, were thinking, *Roger, give it a rest, leave the kid alone,* Roger gave him a bit of a shake and told him, "I think you are.
>
> "I think you're stronger than you think.

"I think you're stronger than all of us.

"But that doesn't mean you can't cry, that doesn't mean you can't be sad.

"Only really strong guys like you and me know it's okay to be sad and it's okay to cry, but we still have to be strong, right?"

And Roger gathers Tyrone into a life-affirming bear hug as the boy agrees that life has to go on. Or that life is for the living. Or that you can't give up. Or whatever it is that this clichéd but still powerful scene communicates to us about human existence.[25]

In all sorts of stories and songs and speeches and sermons, we are invited to get back on our feet, to fight another round, to never never never give in. That makes us human, we're told, that we rebound from adversity, that we keep on going when (presumably) some other species would metaphorically throw in the towel. As stirring and necessary as this human truth may be, however, whether it comes to us from rock music or Winston Churchill, whether it is expressed by a real-life rape survivor or a character in a zombie story, the truth is that tenacity in the face of difficulty does not differentiate us from zombies, who also can be knocked down and get back up again.

In *Shaun of the Dead*, the Queen song "Don't Stop Me Now" is played during a battle scene, and although it seems on its face to offer the same message of tenacity, part of the comic genius of the scene is that it is unclear exactly to whom the lyrics "Don't stop me now" are meant to be applied. Is it to Shaun and his mates, struggling to take down a zombie who has attacked them in their safe haven, the Winchester? Or is it the zombified pub owner, who shrugs off a series of violent attacks and continues to trudge after them? The truth is, it can be applied to both. Human beings don't give up, or, at least, they shouldn't. But zombies don't give up, either. That is "zombie nature."

A powerful section of the novel *World War Z* recounts the Battle of Yonkers, where professional soldiers employed some of the most advanced weaponry on the planet against the unending stream of zombies and they kept coming. Despite artillery, tanks, automatic weapons, even tactical bombing, the zombies ("Zack" in military lingo) don't stop. After fighters drop ordinance that shakes the earth and knocks the defenders to their own knees, the soldiers look up, and what they see is chilling: "And then they came, right out of the smoke like a freakin' little kid's nightmare. Some were steaming, some were even still burning... some were walking, some crawling, some just dragging themselves along on their torn bellies."[26] It is the human soldiers who break in the face of this unstoppable horde; the soldiers turn and run, and, of course, the zombies pursue them, walking, crawling, and dragging themselves.

Zombies' ability to rebound from punishment and their seeming tenacity amaze both the characters who encounter them and ourselves as viewers and readers, no matter how well we know the zombie mythos. In *Afterlife with Archie*, zombie Jughead crashes the Riverdale Halloween Party and attacks Ethel Muggs. Ethel then, amazingly, stands and lunges for Betty and Veronica, who knocks Ethel's head sideways with the fire extinguisher. But Ethel gets back to her feet again, her head now hanging limply to one side. As a by-stander notes, "head's up, gang. Ethel Muggs... nowhere near dead."[27] In a later scene from the first story arc, Archie is forced to turn on his reanimated father to save himself and

his mother, and although he attacks the zombie with a baseball bat and sends him crashing down the stairs, zombie Dad
is still hungry for more. In one of the most emotionally powerful scenes of its kind, a weeping Archie is forced to smash the
zombie again and again until its brain is destroyed and at last
it lies still.[28]

In *Shaun of the Dead*, zombie persistence is played more
for laughs than for emotion. Mary, the first zombie who arrives in Shaun's backyard, falls onto a post sticking up from
the ground, impaling herself. It would be certain death for a
human, but Mary inches her way up off the post, turns toward
the appalled Shaun and Ed, and the camera actually shoots
through the gaping hole in her body as she returns to the
attack. It is their—and our—introduction to their resilience.
Clearly, surviving these creatures will not be easy. In *28 Days
Later*, victims of the virus have incredible powers of pursuit;
the fast zombies can outlast and even outrun their prey. In
Marvel Zombies, the zombified heroes are in various states of
impossible disarray and decrepitude—Spiderman has lost a
leg, the Hulk is split open from the inside, and Iron Man is
literally cut in half at the waist—yet they go right on eating.
Like all zombies, the former heroes are driven not by the
human spirit, but by hunger. Their biological imperatives are
less noble, certainly, but they have the same result.

They don't stop.

They never never never never never give up.

But if motion and tenacity do not mean we are alive,
what does? What constitutes the difference between us and
the shape under the sheet, the decaying corpse lurching
toward us with arms outstretched? Certainly it must include
more than carpe diem, more than an awareness that one is
called to live fully and completely, although for many of us,

Shaun, Ed, and Liz included, a little more awareness might be a valuable thing marking us as human. Wisdom teachings from many traditions extol mindfulness as a central feature of being alive, whether it is the concept of mindfulness made famous in the West by the Buddhist monk Thích Nhất Hạnh ("Mindfulness is like that—it is the miracle which can call back in a flash our dispersed mind and restore it to wholeness so that we can live each minute of life") or the call to awareness made by Jesus throughout the Christian Gospels. ("If anyone has ears to hear, let him hear.")[29]

In *Shaun of the Dead*, *Zombieland*, and many other stories, one of the ironies is that before the Zombie Apocalypse, most of the human characters weren't completely alive and certainly weren't completely aware. A central comic conceit of *Shaun of the Dead* is that, given how sunk in unawareness most of the living have become, it takes them a substantial length of time to notice that the dead are literally walking the earth. Shaun and Ed watch uncomprehending as a zombie woman tears into a human man outside the Winchester; instead of seeing an attack, they see an embrace. Something similar takes place in a flashback in *Zombieland* when Columbus (Jesse Eisenberg) welcomes his attractive neighbor, 406 (Amber Heard) into his apartment and, mistaking her attacks for amorous advances, doesn't seem to notice that she has turned into a zombie until it is almost too late. He finally has to brain (debrain?) her with the toilet lid and still doesn't seem to understand what has happened.

In *Pride and Prejudice and Zombies*, the perpetually dim Reverend Mr. Collins seems unable to see that his wife has been attacked by "the unmentionables" (the zombies in this mythos) and is slowly becoming one of them. When friend and protagonist Elizabeth Bennet comes to visit the Collinses, she finds herself "greatly distressed" by her friend Charlotte's appearance: "It had been months since she had seen Charlotte, and kind months they had not been, for her friend's skin was now quite gray and marked with sores, and her speech appallingly labored. That none of the others noticed this, Elizabeth attributed to their stupidity—particularly Mr. Collins, who apparently had no idea that his wife was "three-quarters dead."[30] Admittedly, mistaken identity is a familiar comic trope, and thus we might expect to find it more often in zombie comedies (zom-coms) than in straight zombie drama (zom-dram?), but it is typical of the zombie narrative that survivors will put their heads in the sand and somehow avoid recognizing what is happening right in front of them. Even in more serious versions of the story, someone refuses to believe what is happening—or tells himself or herself a continuing untruth as a way of dealing with the situation, a psychological state known as avoidance coping.[31] In the novel *World War Z*, for example, a smuggler tells how in the early stages of the outbreak, families would often attempt to restrain loved ones as though they were alive and sentient: "Their family usually had them bound and gagged. You'd see something moving in the back of a car, squirming softly under clothing or heavy blankets. You'd hear banging from a car's boot, or, later, from crates with airholes in the backs of vans. Airholes....they really didn't know what was happening to their loved ones."[32] Didn't know—or couldn't accept? Buddhists speak of "Right View," one of the elements of the Eightfold Path to enlightenment; the fact that this wisdom must be taught suggests it does not come naturally to us, this seeing things as they are without illusions or preconceptions.

Other zombie stories illustrate the difficulty of this "Right View." In *The Walking Dead* comic, Rick discovers that the farmer with whom he and the group have taken shelter, Hershel, has been keeping his son and other zombies shut away in his barn. When Rick confronts Hershel, the response is classic denial. After his son Shawn turned, Hershel says, "I didn't know what else to do. So I kept Shawn in the barn.... But I couldn't kill him. I couldn't bring myself to do that." When Rick tries to tell Hershel that the walking corpse in the barn is no longer Shawn, Hershel explodes: "What made you such a goddamn expert? I don't know about you, but the zombies around here didn't come with a fucking instruction manual! We don't know a goddamn thing about them. We don't know what they're thinking—what they're feeling. We don't know if it's a disease or side effects of some kind of chemical warfare. We don't know shit! For all we know these things could wake up tomorrow, heal up, and be completely normal again."[33] It hardly needs to be said that this resurrection and reunion is never going to happen, at least not in the way Hershel hopes, yet he wants so badly to believe that it might that he endangers himself, his surviving family, and Rick's community. Not surprisingly, this failure to confront reality returns to haunt him when the dead locked up in the barn get free and attack.

Another example of denial comes in a flashback in *The Road*. McCarthy depicts "the man," the book's main character, in conversation with his late wife, who chides him for being in denial. When he tells her "We're survivors," she flatly contradicts him. "What in God's name are you talking about? We're not survivors. We're the walking dead in a horror film." After the apocalyptic turn—the book never states precisely what happens, although the ash, fires, and growing cold might suggest some sort of nuclear event—the man, his wife, and their son remain at their home as the world outside falls apart. After many nights talking over her options, the woman elects suicide—and says they ought to kill the boy as well. Although the man responds, "That's crazy talk," she disagrees.

"No. I'm speaking the truth. Sooner or later they will catch us and they will kill us. They will rape me. They'll rape him. They are going to rape us and kill us and eat us and you won't face it."[34]

These apocalyptic narratives illustrate two ways of facing the terrible events that characters have experienced. One can be hopeful, which, taken to its extreme, becomes delusion. One can be resigned to the way things seem, which when pushed too far can become despair. Perhaps the key is to see things as they are, not to live in despair or delusion but to accept and name reality and to offer appropriate reactions to it. In *Shaun of the Dead*, Shaun initially protests when Ed uses the word "zombie": "The zed-word. Don't say it!" But then he turns his head and sees some: "Oh no. There they are." Similarly in *Scouts Guide to the Zombie Apocalypse*, when Ben (Tye Sheridan) sees a man with a hole blown in his chest stagger back to his feet, there's only one possible conclusion for what is happening: "Yup. Zombie." From that point of recognition, something can be done, some action taken, and the characters can move forward with appropriate plans.

Some would argue that lack of awareness about and lack of involvement in our own lives is part and parcel of living in a consumerist society, but it may be that these things are simply part and parcel of being human. Buddhists and Benedictines alike would not have to preach mindfulness and attention to each moment if mindfulness and attention were not sorely missing from the average consciousness.

Perhaps many of us are missing out on life because of our distraction and lack of connection. But this modern disconnection becomes a luxury that cannot be sustained during the Zombie Apocalypse. Robert Kirkman notes in his introduction to volume 1 of *The Walking Dead* comic: "In a world ruled by the dead, we are forced to finally start living."[35] It's no longer enough to be in motion without noticing, to simply consume mindlessly; even zombies can do that.

STAYING ALIVE

Staying alive's as good as it gets.
—SELENA (NAOMIE HARRIS), *28 Days Later*

Perhaps you recall that the warrior Conan (Arnold Schwarzenegger), when asked "What is good in life?" answers, "To crush your enemies, to see them driven before you, and to hear the lamentations of their women," but surely this response is particular to a certain kind of culture. It wouldn't be my answer about what life is about or, probably, yours. I'd respond, "Life with my family. A great Hong Kong action film. A long hike in the mountains. A good church service that concludes with taking the Eucharist. A cold gin and tonic at the end of a long day's work." You might have similar—or radically different—answers. So what are universal truths about what matters in life? And what ultimately makes us human?

Religious and epistemological responses to this question might begin by considering that what defines us as human is the soul, spirit, or *anima*. As writer-producer Angela Kang has noted, humans have them; zombies don't. Pope Benedict—

:

formerly the noted theologian Joseph Ratzinger—wrote that "for other creatures who are not called to eternity, death means solely the end of existence on earth."[36] Perhaps dogs—or dolphins—do have intelligence and some form of awareness. But most theologians would argue that only humans have eternal souls. Zombies do not. Their essence is now solely physical, not spiritual.

The perplexing element of zombies, though, as I've noted, is that they bear outward resemblance to the humans they once were. They walk. They consume. They reproduce, after a fashion. But when we speak of the soul, we are speaking of more than just an animating force. We are speaking of a separate, spiritual component possessed by human beings. When the zombie dies, that spiritual essence departs the body, just as it would any corpse. When, for example, Shaun tells his mother that the monster trapped in their car is not his stepfather, part of what he means is that what remains is only Philip's animal, physical being. The creature in the car is soulless. That which made Philip Philip has fled that decaying carcass, and only the physical semblance of his stepfather is left.

Later, when Shaun's mum succumbs to a bite, Shaun relives this conversation, this time as the one needing to be convinced. "Don't point that gun at my mum!" he yells, although his mother is dead, and the snarling, cowl-eyed creature that stands up as they are arguing is, like Philip, soulless, animated only in the most basic sense of the word. It moves. It eats. But it most definitely is not human.

Philosophers and theologians have different explanations for the *anima*/soul/pneuma that differentiates human beings from other organisms. Aristotle asks in his treatise on the soul, "What is the soul of plant, animal, man?" He goes on to conclude that while all living creatures have souls, their types of soul may be described as functioning in different ways. In plants, for example, the soul is capable of growth and reproduction; animals have this vegetative soul as well as a meditative soul, giving them powers of mobility and perception. Humans, at the top of Aristotle's spiritual *scala naturae*, bear these lesser elements of soul as well as Logos, that which gives them the power of reason and thought.[37] With the rare exceptions I've noted, zombies do not reason and think; part of how we know we are alive is our ability to do so.

Descartes, who famously concluded "I think, therefore I am," founded Cartesian dualism, the principle that body and soul (or consciousness) are separate. It is one thing to say you are alive; it is yet another thing to say you are sentient. Perhaps we could apply this dualism to the two Philips in *Shaun of the Dead*: the first one, apologizing to Shaun in the back of the Jaguar, has both animation and sentience. In his final moments and last words, Philip is consciously trying to explain something to Shaun and to offer him some much-needed comfort and resolution. After he dies and is transformed into a ghoul, zombie Philip has animation but (with the possibly coincidental incidence of his turning off the radio) no sentience. Moments earlier he had been acting out of humane and deeply generous motives, now he operates only out of animal hunger. Whatever generosity and humanity were inside that form, they are gone. It is a powerful representation of the notion that soul or spirit departs the body at death.

In the Hebrew and Christian traditions, humankind is formed in the image of God, *imago dei*. In the first Creation story presented in the Book of Genesis, readers learn that God pronounced "Let us make humankind in our image, according to our likeness."[38] The creation of birds, fish, and animals is described in earlier verses, and while God looks at them and sees those creations as good, only humans are said to be made with the express imprint of God. Only humans are made in the divine image. Later sections of the scriptures—and generations of Jewish and Christian theologians—explored ramifications of "image" and "likeness" and argued about the reasons for the Fall and why, if human beings are made in the image of God, they are not God. But for all these thinkers, the spark of divinity that marks humankind as in God's image is a differentiating element. Humans are born with that spark; it departs from their bodies when they die. Zombies are made in the image of humankind, but because they are dead, they cannot sustain the *imago dei*.

Admittedly, some philosophers argue that there is no soul. Gilbert Ryle, a philosopher who taught at Oxford, took on what he considered "the dogma of the Ghost in the Machine" in his book *The Concept of Mind,* and his work launched a wave of discussion on the material view of consciousness, which is that there is no soul and that all elements of consciousness can be attached to the body and to physiological impulses.[39] Contemporary materialists echo the argument that the soul is a myth—or a superstition. A recent post on the Richard Dawkins Foundation website bears the simple headline "It's Time to Abandon the Irrational Concept of a Soul."[40] In his 2007 preface to *The God Illusion,* Dawkins himself wrote that "the comfort that religion seems to offer is founded on the neurologically highly implausible premise that we survive the death of our brains."[41] For Dawkins, as a materialist, all bodily characteristics are physical, the mind or soul cannot be separated from the brain and its activity, and thus, all consciousness dies at the death of the physical body. This too would account for a distinction between the living human and the walking dead; the biological processes and impulses that we might understand as our higher humanity, our "soul," cease once the brain ceases to function as a living seat of consciousness. Although the brain is symbolically important as the center of the zombie's vulnerability, the Romero zombie does not have the processes that might account for pity, self-sacrifice, altruism, or any of the other actions and reactions we associate with the soul, spirit, or highest human impulses.

Whether we approach the question as religious believers or as materialists, then, zombies cannot replicate the higher functions of human existence. Moreover, in most mythos, they cannot even solve simple problems or reason their way past booby-traps and roadblocks. (The zombie comedy *Scouts Guide to the Zombie Apocalypse* makes humorous exceptions for a zombie who seems to have concluded that he can use a trampoline to reach his prey on a second floor, and another who seems to have some memory of a Britney Spears song.) "The restless," as zombies are called in the comic *The New Deadwardians*, are easily confined behind fences and gates. When Rick and his group discover the fences of the prison in *The Walking Dead*, they believe that once they have cleared out the walkers inside they will be able to live in safety from those on the outside. In *Shaun of the Dead*, zombies can be foiled by locking bathroom doors and erecting barricades, just as in the various versions of *I Am Legend*, the hero hides out safely from the undead monsters, whether inside his reinforced house, as in Richard Matheson's original novel, or inside a security-enhanced brownstone in the Will Smith film. Even the zombies who overrun the Israeli defenses in the movie version of *World War Z* do so without benefit of reason. They swarm the walls like insects, and eventually enough of them clamber up the squirming mass to plummet to the other side.

Taking advantage of the fact that the living dead lack the power of reason, *The Zombie Survival Guide* offers dozens of practical ways to zombie-proof one's home or hideout, ranging from "Demolish the staircase! As zombies are unable to climb, this method guarantees your safety" to "grab whatever supplies you can, take hold of a weapon, and climb onto the roof. If the ladder is kicked away and there is no direct access…the undead will be unable to reach you."[42] Although they will keep coming if they sense prey, they cannot formulate attack plans or solve problems and, like herd animals, will follow their fellows off a cliff or directly into mortal danger.

In the graphic novel *Recorded Attacks*, Max Brooks writes of an infestation in second-century Scotland in which a Roman commander dug trenches, filled them with crude oil, set it on fire, and left only a tiny patch of land through which they could pass, allowing his much smaller force of legionnaires to decapitate the entire horde or force them into the burning oil. In another recorded encounter from the nineteenth century, a French Foreign Legion outpost in northern Africa was besieged by hundreds, perhaps thousands, of ghouls. Ammunition, food, and sanity vanished as the creatures milled about seeking entrance. At last, the commander hatched a desperate plan: after his men lured all the zombies to the front gate, he opened it, led them inside, and was pulled to safety as his men escaped over the walls. The gate was shut, leaving the zombies trapped in the fort's courtyard, where they remain to this day, now bones withered by the punishing desert sun.[43] Any reasoning creature would have avoided these obvious traps, but the zombies perished by the thousands; unlike the military in *World War Z*'s Battle of Yonkers, these human defenders formulated proper responses to the living dead and implemented them to perfection.

If reflection, conscious thought, and self-awareness are a large part of what makes us human (and the lack of which marks zombies as inhuman), a sense of purpose may be another defining difference. Zombies have drives and biological imperatives: they attack, and in most stories, they feed. As *The Zombie Survival Guide* notes, however, they do not think, communicate, or plan, although they do proceed inexorably toward their prey. The hordes of undead milling around outside the farmhouse in *Night of the Living Dead*, the mindless walkers of *The Walking Dead*, the African zombies of *Last Ones Out*, the "unmentionables" of *Pride and Prejudice and Zombies*, and the running zombies of *28 Days Later* and the film *World War Z* all have one impulse driving them forward.

The newscaster in *Night of the Living Dead* shares the startling news that "all persons who die during this crisis from whatever cause will come back to life to seek human victims, unless their bodies are first disposed of by cremation." Similarly, at the beginning of *Dawn of the Dead*, zombie expert Dr. Foster (David Crawford) says on the news that "every dead body that is not exterminated becomes one of them. It gets up and kills! The people it kills get up and kill!" He explains their drive in this way: "They kill for one reason: they kill for food. They eat their victims, you understand that, Mr. Berman? That's what keeps them going!"

The 1985 film *Return of the Living Dead*, directed by Dan O'Bannon, is famous for introducing zombies' attraction to brains. The way it is explained is both chilling and heartbreaking. In an exchange between a zombie (Cherry Davis) and Ernie (Don Calfa), this is what emerges:

ERNIE KALTENBRUNNER:	Why do you eat people?
1/2 WOMAN CORPSE:	Not people. Brains.
ERNIE KALTENBRUNNER:	Brains only?
1/2 WOMAN CORPSE:	Yes.
ERNIE KALTENBRUNNER:	Why?
1/2 WOMAN CORPSE:	The pain!
ERNIE KALTENBRUNNER:	What about the pain?
1/2 WOMAN CORPSE:	The pain of being dead!
ERNIE KALTENBRUNNER:	It hurts…to be dead.
1/2 WOMAN CORPSE:	I can feel myself rot.
ERNIE KALTENBRUNNER:	Eating brains…How does that make you feel?
1/2 WOMAN CORPSE:	It makes the pain go away!

Although her severed head is no longer even connected to a body, the Wasp, one of the sentient Marvel zombies, also feels pain. She keeps asking her captor, the Black Panther, for a taste, just the merest nibble of his flesh. Because she can reflect on her condition in ways that zombies normally cannot, she can provide us one of the most useful glimpses of "what keeps them going." It is hunger, sheer unwavering hunger:

> "You don't understand what it's like. I need to feed. I—can't think straight. The hungrier I get, the more the hunger consumes me.
> "It's hard to explain—the craving—the need—I ache to taste your flesh. I'm starving for it. I'm in pain."[44]

She and the other Marvel zombies, while sentient, have that hunger in common with all zombies. Likewise, Liv, the titular protagonist of *iZombie*, possesses thought and a conscience, but she too must eat brains to survive, and this drive forces her to shape her life around eating as well, although at least she is able to take her drive and derive some good from it: "I wanted to do something with my life. I wanted to help people. Not, necessarily, as a zombie psychic who eats murder victim brains, but still." Unlike Jan and Liv, other zombies, of course, do not think, they do not plan. But when they sense food, particularly human flesh, they move unerringly toward it.

In many stories, a moment comes when humans must pretend to be zombies, which reveals something about the distinctions between us. Perhaps, as in *The Walking Dead*, characters drape themselves with entrails, putting on the equivalent of a zombie suit. In the first arc of the comic, Rick and Glenn (portrayed by Steven Yeun on the TV show) stuff severed zombie limbs in their pockets and cover themselves with their gore. Rick has been wondering what it is that allows zombies to locate living humans and concludes that it must be smell. Clearly, he says, it's not movement, or the fact that zombies and humans both (typically) have arms and legs. "It should be easy for them to mix us up," he says, "but they never seem to attack each other."[45] In this mythos, smell seems to be the key. Rick and Glenn are safe in their raid into Atlanta. They aren't given away by their conversation, or even by their wheeling a shopping cart full of guns and ammunition, until a thunderstorm comes and the downpour washes away their awful scent. It is then that the zombies awake to their difference, and they barely escape.

Shaun of the Dead, as we might expect, plays this survival trope for laughs. When it becomes clear that they can't get to the pub where they hope to find safety because of the throng of zombies, the characters practice their zombie moans, their thousand-yard stares, their seized-up motions, coached by Dianne (Lucy Davis): "Look at the face. It's vacant. With a hint of sadness." They try out, although Ed at first refuses, saying, "I'll do it on the night." Perhaps it shouldn't work, but it seems to; Shaun and his mates lurch down the street to the door of the Winchester, terrified but seemingly unnoticed. They are ultimately revealed as human nonzombies not by their odors or their Off-Broadway moans; they are given away only when Ed takes out his cell phone and answers a call from an old mate.

WHY WE LIVE

> Nowadays, you breathe and you risk your life. The
> only thing you can choose is what you risk it for.
>
> — HERSHEL GREENE, "Isolation," *The Walking Dead*

Ed's example notwithstanding, one of the things human beings possess is the ability to suppress cravings, to redirect hungers, and to make decisions rationally, not based on perceived need. We have the ability to feel empathy and compassion. We can choose self-sacrifice over selfishness. We can choose, in a very real sense, a higher purpose. Like Liz in *Shaun of the Dead*, we can conclude that there is more to life than sitting in the Winchester and simply consuming beer and crisps: we are called to do something more.

Robert Kirkman said that *The Walking Dead* is, in some ways, a thought experiment. What do people turn into when they are given the freedom to be whatever they choose? Angela Kang likewise told me that the show is about survival and about what people are willing to do to survive. What do we do when our biological impulses war with our ethical impulses? In some cases they will produce things like the apparent sanctuary Terminus, where the inhabitants devour those who have arrived there seeking asylum, against all rules of decency and hospitality, or show us Rick in such emotional and moral turmoil that he oscillates back and forth between the self-sacrificing peace officer who didn't even want to pull his weapon when we first met him to the Ricktator, the character who in the season 5 episode "Try" alarms Deanna (Tovah Feldshuh) and the citizens of Alexandria by raving about how "We know what needs to be done and we do it.... If you don't fight, you die."

In a notable speech from season 5's episode "Them," Rick retells a story about his grandfather, a World War II veteran, and how he got through the war by convincing himself he was already dead: "And then after a few years of pretending he was dead...he made it out alive.... This is how we survive. We tell ourselves...that we are the walking dead." As in the poem of World War I veteran Wilfred Owen, you survive the shelling by becoming dead while you yet live.

But at the same time, this human laboratory also produces the opposite, characters who move from dark places where we find them to more ethical and enlightened positions. Before the events of *The Walking Dead*, Daryl Dixon was a survivalist of no fixed domicile, a drifter who seems already well adapted to the chaos and violence that has arrived with the Zombie Apocalypse. He and his brother Merle (Michael Rooker) are survivors, plain and simple. But during the course of the story, he too has demonstrated change, so much so that a CNN story about the show was titled, after a popular Internet meme, "If Daryl Dies We Riot," and the YouTube video "The Transformation of Daryl Dixon" has commanded a million and a half views as of the writing of this book.[46] Norman Reedus told CNN's Henry Hanks that he has seen a huge evolution in Daryl's character: "He's starting to make connections with people for the first time. The relationships he's forming with these people and this feeling that people need him. I think he feels good about it. He hates what's going on and people can die any second, but at the same time, he's finding things out about himself."[47]

It is Daryl who pushes back against Rick's speech in "Them" saying that the survivors are the walking dead. "We ain't them," he says, and then repeats it. Although he has come originally from a much darker place than Rick, it is he who holds onto his humanity and his sanity. In the season 3 episode "When the Dead Come Knocking," for example, we find Daryl embracing a new role: caretaker, even rescuer. He swoops back into the prison on his bike with baby food for the as-yet-unnamed Baby Judith, takes her in his arms, and croons to her as he feeds her from a bottle. When Rick thanks him for saving his infant daughter, Daryl responds in words that demonstrate the power of transformation: "It's what we do."

As I'll explore in more detail in chapter 3, "It's what we do" is a defining human notion. As Desmond Tutu (himself the witness of some of the best and the worst that humanity can choose) puts it, to be human is about the ability to make moral choices. "God," he says, "created us freely, for freedom. To be human in the understanding of the Bible is to be free to choose, free to choose to love or to hate, to be kind or to be cruel. To be human is to be a morally responsible creature, and more responsibility is a nonsense when the person in fact is not free to choose from several available options....It is part of being created in the image of God, this freedom that can make us into glorious creatures or damn us into hellish ones."[48] Rowan Williams describes our humanity in similar terms, noting that in the Judeo-Christian story, "creation comes to a sort of climax point when God makes something that reflects him more fully than anything else—beings capable of choice and of love."[49] This image of humanity being centered in choice and love is also reflected in the Jesus depicted by the historic creeds, which wrestle with the confusion around Jesus's dual nature, fully divine and yet fully one of us. As one version of the Nicene Creed says, through the power of God the Spirit and his human mother, Mary, Jesus came down from heaven "and became truly human." In accomplishing this, Christians believe, God took up moral choice, the possibility of failure, the necessity of reaching accommodations with pain and death, and the closest possible identification with humanity. That Jesus consistently chose the welfare of others over his own is the great testimony of his life and makes him the model of humanity for the rest of us. In Jesus, as Dr. Williams says, we discover "a human being in whom God's action is at work without interruption or impediment."[50]

With all respect to Professor Dawkins and to evolutionary theories of ethics, perhaps what makes us fully human is not naturally hardwired into our cortexes like the sexual and hunger impulses. In a recent radio conversation, British religion scholar Linda Woodhead told me that it's not natural for people to be self-sacrificing and talked about how humans have to learn those behaviors. So-called liberal values, she said, are "not the most natural ones.... We have to be schooled and socialized and educated into believing every human being counts for something, because it does not come naturally to us."[51] One part of our humanity, the part that Archbishop Tutu equated with the hellish, is purely self-serving, hungry, acquisitive, without regard to the needs or desires of others. It is this part of us, we might say, that is actually closest to the zombie's essential nature and is the least human part of our human nature.

But when we see men and women giving away what they possess, when we see them caring less about their own needs and desires than the needs of others, we see a higher humanity, of which zombies are incapable. In the bravery of that French Legion officer who risks his life in trapping the zombies to preserve his men, in the Wildling mother who sacrifices herself so that her children can escape Hardhome, in Shaun's willingness to lead zombies away from Liz and his friends despite the danger, in Glenn's willingness to sneak into Atlanta again and again seeking supplies for his community, we see most clearly the ways we differ from the living dead—and most powerfully, the things of which human beings are capable.

Which, again, is not to say that they necessarily come easily to human beings. We have to be taught these things that we think make us human, whether by parents or by priests. In most faith traditions—as well as in the ethical teachings of atheists—we find a set of calls to self-restraint, self-sacrifice, and self-giving that are absolutely not biologically based. In Buddhism we find the call to Right Action among the elements of the Eightfold Path. Right Action includes living in harmony and in peace with one's fellow human beings, not stealing or killing, avoiding overindulgence in sensual or sexual pleasures, and living honestly. These teachings demand a conscious willingness to take less for ourselves than we can—perhaps even less than we want—in the name of right action.

Among the Five Pillars of Islam, we find Zakat, the call to charity. Every Muslim (that is, every person who seeks to submit to Allah/God) is taught to devote a percentage of his or her resources to helping others who are less fortunate. Why should anyone do this? It doesn't benefit us or our families, and so a call to charity seems like a counterintuitive use of our resources. But it does benefit the world, whether we give to those around us or those who are part of the larger human family. Islam also contains the concept of the jihad, often misunderstood both by adherents and by those outside the tradition. It is the lesser jihad, the conflict against those who are the presumed foes of Islam, that steals headlines when evil men and women kill innocents in its name. More important by far is the greater jihad, the lifelong struggle against evil and our own worst natures. It is this battle that matters most in terms of our own souls.

Within Judaism, the Hebrew Bible contains dozens of calls to recognize and support the needs of the poor, the widow, the orphan, and the alien—that is, all of those sorts of people who most need the help of generous and compassionate neighbors. This too is a form of lifelong struggle against evil and selfishness. One of many such prophetic calls appears in the Book of Jeremiah:

> Thus says the LORD: Go down to the house of the king of Judah, and speak there this word, and say: Hear the word of the LORD, O King of Judah sitting on the throne of David—you, and your servants, and your people who enter these gates.
>
> Thus says the LORD: Act with justice and righteousness, and deliver from the hand of the oppressor anyone who has been robbed. And do no wrong or violence to the alien, the orphan, and the widow, or shed innocent blood in this place.
>
> For if you will indeed obey this word, then through the gates of this house shall enter kings who sit on the throne of David, riding in chariots and on horses, they, and their servants, and their people.

> But if you will not heed these words, I swear by myself,
> says the LORD, that this house shall become a desolation.[52]

In the Hebrew Testament, prophetic calls for right behavior are accompanied by the promise of reward for self-sacrifice and of punishments for satisfying one's appetites for wealth and possessions. Justice, or righteousness, comes from a consciousness of one's place, the principle that our common humanity binds us together and that none are to be ignored.

We observe this Jewish call to help and support others in much of the Christian Testament and see it expressed perhaps most powerfully in the parable of the Good Samaritan, which Jesus tells in response to a question about whom we are commanded to love by the Jewish laws, that is: Who is our neighbor? As Jesus tells the story, a Jewish traveler is beaten by thieves and left for dead by the side of the road. Two religious leaders from his own tradition pass by and, seeing him lying there, move quickly away, afraid, perhaps, that they will become the next victims. Finally, a traditional enemy of the Jews, a Samaritan, stops and despite the possible danger helps the wounded man, carries him to an inn so he can rest and heal, and pays for his lodging. Jesus's lesson is clear enough in the story, yet he asks the initial questioner "Who was a neighbor to the fallen man?"

"The one who helped him," comes the grudging reply.

"Go and do the same" is what Jesus says as a closing response.[53] In the Christian tradition, as in these others, compassion toward those in need is commanded of us. That it is not a natural response is seen in the fact that the two religious leaders, people who knew the Hebrew law and were servants of the people, were more moved by their personal safety than by their ethical callings. But that it is a possible response is demonstrated by the fact that the Samaritan, even though he knows that the wounded Jew probably looks down on and despises him, nonetheless does the difficult and necessary work of compassion. Augustine, in musing on this parable, expanded the initial question from "Who then is my neighbor" by blasting out the boundaries. All human beings are our neighbors, he taught, and thus although we bear a special responsibility for those we encounter in the course of our day-to-day travels, our neighbors are all people everywhere.[54] Wherever someone is in need, our compassion should be directed toward them. As the poet and priest John Donne wrote, "no man is an island," but each of us is part of a common humanity, and the death or desecration of any of us is a blight on us all.[55]

This is a hard teaching indeed, but it and like teachings have been embraced often enough throughout history for us to see a sharp contrast between the zombies, hungry and unable to govern their impulses, and human beings, subject to the same physical impulses but capable of subverting and even submerging them for the sake of others. In the story "Escape from the Mall" when Tyrone's father wades into a swarm of zombies to save his son, or in *Afterlife with Archie* when Archie leaves a safe haven to return to Riverdale and see if his parents are alive, we see people pushing past fear, pushing aside danger, and embracing higher concepts of humanity.

These elements of self-abnegation can be seen to have a larger scope in such stories as the transformation of Tomanuga Ijiro in the novel *World War Z*. Tomanuga is the self-loathing Japanese blinded by the American atomic bomb who becomes a warrior monk and the gardener of Japan after it is abandoned because of the zombie infestation. After leaving his job as a hotel gardener, he took up residence (guided, he says, by the traditional Shinto gods of Japan, the *kami*) in the mountains of Hokkaido, Japan's most northern island, where he learned how to fight off the living dead and how that ongoing battle was a part of his vocation. Tomanuga describes the moment when his purpose at last became clear to him and how he took on an apprentice in the sacrificial work to which the gods had called him: "I explained that, like any garden, Japan could not be allowed to wither and die. We would care for her, we would preserve her, we would annihilate the walking blight that infested and defiled her and we would restore her beauty and purity for the day when her children would return to her."[56]

Why? Because this is what we do.

Not because we simply need to save ourselves, but because at the heart of what we are, we are called to save others. Ultimately, we might say that it is this impulse, whether we call it the actions that emerge from our conscience or soul or deepest humanity, that most powerfully separates human beings from zombies and marks us as living beings. At our worst, we share all the worst features of those inhuman monsters and compound them with our consciousness. But at our best, we rise above our own hungers, our impulses, even our own potential destruction and try to do the right thing.

At the end of the Will Smith version of *I Am Legend*, his Robert Neville sacrifices himself not only so that a mother and her child can escape, but in order that humanity can be saved from the viral epidemic. As Anna (Alice Braga) recaps his contribution in voiceover at the movie's end, she has recourse to Neville's beloved Bob Marley, who sang that we should sing songs of redemption, that we should "Light up the darkness": "In 2009, a deadly virus burned through our civilization, pushing humankind to the edge of extinction." Neville's research found an answer; his courage and his sacrifice made it possible for that research to reach those who could use it to save the world. "We are his legacy. This is his legend.... Light up the darkness."

Although the Marvel Comics character Deadpool is usually played for self-referential laughs, in his version of the Marvel zombies story we discover a surprising amount of sacrificial heroism. Like other stories of the Zombie Apocalypse, the one in the Deadpool stories concerns a world overrun with the undead, and as humans retell the story in *Return of the Living Deadpool*, that story sounds like this: "The undead swarmed across the world like a disease. They hungered for the death of the living. And the beauty and prosperity and peace that was civilization fell before the horde. But the world struggled against the swelling numbers of the dead. And— brothers and sisters—the planet's immune system spat up the merc with a mouth to purge the zombie infection. One man striving to save all of mankind."[57] Now if you have read Deadpool comics or seen the hit movie, you probably know that "altruism" and "Deadpool" are words that rarely appear in the same sentence. This mercenary with a mouth seems, in fact, to be defined by self-gratification, whether through his love of chimichangas, through his omnivorous sexuality, or simply through his inability to stop loving the sound of his own voice. But in this apocalyptic narrative, Deadpool offers himself up for the life of the world, not just in this history, but in the action of the comic itself. Toward the end, when he is told that the only way to stop the tide of zombie Deadpools now washing over the world as a result of the earlier Deadpool's well-intentioned but misguided action (take Zombie Apocalypse, add Deadpool's healing factor, and shake) is for him to enter an experimental machine and offer his life to end the lives of all his alter egos, he agrees. His friend Liz objects, but Deadpool, in true hero fashion, comforts her, saying, "Believe me...it sucks. But I think this is what I'm meant to do. I think that's why I'm different from the others. I think that's why I met you. Liz...I'm sorry, kid. But I've got a chance to make the world a better place."[58]

Perhaps no version of the Zombie Apocalypse illustrates the human capacity to choose sacrifice more formally than the story of the Night's Watch in the Song of Ice and Fire/*Game of Thrones* saga. Because of the swirl of political intrigue, sex, and violence that makes up the Game of Thrones, we, like the characters in these stories, sometimes lose track of the true menace to Westeros: the wights and the White Walkers who animate them. But the human wars and machinations are only distractions from the coming winter; as red priestess Melisandre (Carice van Houten) says in the season 5 episode "Sons of the Harpy," ultimately "there's only one war: life against death." Both books and TV stories begin by laying out in chilling terms the menace of the living dead, and during the course of the larger story, it becomes increasingly clear to Jon Snow, who is first a Brother and later Lord Commander of the Night's Watch, that the towering Wall with its magical wards must have been built for more than to keep marauding Wildlings out. Like others in the story, he has seen the dead walk, he has seen brothers violently enlisted into the undead army, and he begins to understand what his vows truly mean. He and the Brothers of the Night's Watch may be all that stand between the living and the coming Zombie Apocalypse.

Those vows offer a powerful statement of self-sacrifice and perhaps offer us a useful spot to conclude this section on how human beings are marked as human because of their ability to make moral choices that go against their own narrow self-interests. As he and his commander face certain death at the hands of surrounding Wildlings in *A Clash of Kings*, Jon Snow is commanded by Qhorin Halfhand to slay him and to pretend to renounce his vows so that he can join the Wildlings to uncover their strength and their plans. To fortify their wills as each makes a sacrificial choice, Qhorin asks Jon to repeat their vows with him one final time. Those words, repeated across the centuries, are these:

> Night gathers, and now my watch begins. It shall not end until my death. I shall take no wife, hold no lands, father no children. I shall wear no crowns and win no glory. I shall live and die at my post. I am the sword in the darkness. I am the watcher on the walls. I am the fire that burns against the cold, the light that brings the dawn, the horn that wakes the sleepers, the shield that guards the realms of men. I pledge my life and honor to the Night's Watch, for this night and all the nights to come.[59]

This impulse—to carry the light, to light up the darkness, to be the shield that guards the living—is the greatest flowering of our humanity. We often fall short, to be certain. For every Mother Teresa we produce, there seems to be an Adolph Hitler; for every Michonne, a Governor.

But at our best—and thankfully we are sometimes at our best—human beings sing these songs of redemption. Zombies never will. They never could. And at the heart of things, that is an essential difference between us.

We can, and sometimes do, overcome our biology.

Zombies never can and never will.

We differ from zombies in one last essential way. Although they are often found in groups, these are groups of convenience, convened around prey. Human beings are drawn to other human beings not because of biological imperatives to feed, but because we are created or evolved to be social. Every zombie is alone in a crowd, but human beings find themselves and their fullest development in the presence of others like them. In our next chapter we'll look at how zombie narratives explore life in community and how, paradoxically, the end of the world may create powerful and intense gatherings in the face of terror and death.

HUNGRY FOR EACH OTHER

How Zombie Stories Encourage Community

> Sometimes you just want to get together with your friends and kill some zombies.
>
> —CHANDLER GARRETT, *age 17*

> Never Go Off Alone.
>
> —MAX BROOKS, *The Zombie Survival Guide*

MADE FOR COMMUNITY: FROM SOLITUDE TOWARD HOPE

"THAT GUY DOWN there is me."

The movie *Zombieland* opens on a college student named Columbus, alone at night in Garland, Texas, after the Zombie Apocalypse has begun. The camera shows him from high above, emphasizing his loneliness. It is a dark night in a dark world, and Columbus is completely on his own. In voiceover we begin to hear what the movie is truly about—and as usual in a zombie story, it isn't zombies.

In this and many other zombie stories, it's about community.

Why has Columbus made it this far, when so many others have joined the shambling masses? "I may seem like an unlikely survivor," he says, "with all my phobias and my irritable bowel syndrome, but I had the advantage of never having any friends or any close family."

Is this an advantage? Hardly. Like much in *Zombieland*, this is meant as sardonic commentary. Not only is Columbus alone in the world, he is also alone in the parking lot. When he is attacked by first one, then two, then three zombies, he has no one but himself to rely on, nothing but the Rules of Zombieland (for instance, "Cardio," that is, keep yourself in excellent shape) on which to fall back. He outruns the zombies, barely, but his isolation does not bode well for his physical, emotional, or spiritual future. He recognizes that something is missing. "I've always been kind of a loner. I avoided other people like zombies even before they were zombies. Now that they are all zombies, I kind of miss people." The arc of Columbus's character is clearly about community and its central importance to human beings in and out of the Zombie Apocalypse.

In *I Am Legend*, Robert Neville may be the last human left on an earth reshaped by a viral epidemic. At night and in the shadows, Darkseekers roam. Now, Neville walks alone through the streets of New York City, accompanied only by his dog, Sam. Like Tom Hanks's character in *Castaway*, Neville speaks to inanimate objects. In the video store he visits daily, he has set up mannequins so that he can simulate human interaction. He actually begins to become infatuated with one of them, and over a series of days tries to get up the courage to talk to her. And every day he shows up at the meeting site he is announcing on his radio broadcasts, hoping against hope to discover other human survivors.

Like Columbus, Neville is alone when we are first introduced to him, and alienation is also a central theme of *I Am Legend*. As screenwriter Mark Protosevich told me, Neville's isolation was of central importance to the character, and Mark took pains to learn how to accurately depict his condition:

> I did a fair amount of research in regard to people who were
> in circumstances of extreme isolation. Mostly former prison-
> ers that had spent long periods of time in solitary confine-
> ment, as well as hostages who were held by their captors for
> extended amounts of time. I also looked at people who found
> themselves in "survivor" type situations. They had gotten lost
> in the desert, their plane crashed in the mountains, etc. The
> thing that linked all of them? The fear of breaking down psy-
> chologically. The physical challenges were difficult, yes, but
> the real threat was not to the body. It was to the mind. They
> would hallucinate, have suicidal thoughts, paranoid thoughts,
> hostile thoughts, and sink into despair. It was a struggle just
> to function "normally."[1]

Neville's sadness is compounded by grief and loneliness, and when Sam is infected by the virus, Neville can no longer function normally. He goes mad and attacks the Dark-seekers in what could only be described as a suicide mission. Perhaps he decides that he can no longer go on living if he is forced to do it alone. Life outside of community feels like death.

Suicide has to be acknowledged as one of the moral choices open to people in the postapocalyptic world of zombie sto-ries. Neville seems to seek it here, and we find examples in many other iterations of the story: the wife kills herself in *The Road*, a German general chooses that out in the novel *World War Z* after giving orders to leave civilians to die, a family of devout Christians seem to have chosen death by murder-suicide early in *The Walking Dead*, and other characters elect to die in the CDC explosion at the end of the TV show's season 1 rather than continue on in a ravaged world. Many characters in zombie stories reserve suicide as a possible way out. They may hold onto a bullet or two, or have a plan to avoid being taken by the living dead, or by the living, who are sometimes even worse. Shaun has two bullets remaining at the end of *Shaun of the Dead*, although he and Liz, typically, cannot agree about who should be responsible for shooting the other. In *The Walking Dead*, when Rick thinks zombies are going to pull him out from under the tank he has crawled under for shelter, he puts his revolver to his head, but then he sees an opening just above him that he can climb inside. Peter and Francine individually consider suicide at the end of *Dawn of the Dead*. They decide not to kill themselves in the moment, but as they climb into the helicopter to escape, we see something of their fatalistic frame of mind:

> PETER: How much fuel do we have?
> FRANCINE: Not much.
> PETER: All right.

Together they will face their fate, even if that turns out to be death.

In chapter 1, I talked about ways to distinguish the living and the dead. In addition to an animating spirit and the ability to choose against one's own best interests, I noted that the need for community likewise separates zombies and human beings. Zombies may congregate wherever prey is to be found, drawn by smell or alerted by other zombies moaning, but in most stories they do not seek out other zombies. They may not in fact even be aware of each other; in *The New Deadwardians* comic, the dead are invisible to the dead. Yet humans seek other humans, and in those communities, they rise or fall, live or die, together.

One of the tragedies of *Night of the Living Dead* is that in this first story about the attempt to survive a zombie incursion, we see the spectacular failure of a group of people to coalesce as a community. Those gathered inside the farm-house turn on each other, quarrel, hinder rather than support each other. In one short, albeit horrific, night they descend into dissension and chaos, and as they do so, they begin to fall victim to the monsters within, as well as those outside. When Ben (Duane Jones) returns to the house after an abortive escape, Harry attempts to lock him out, and when Ben forces entry, they fight. The result is that Harry is shot and stumbles back down into the cellar to die. Had they worked together, could they all have survived? Perhaps not: Karen's injury would have turned her into a zombie no matter what the rest of the survivors did, and the film shows how easily she killed her mother. But their failure to work together as a community makes it impossible for them to survive.

In the novel *World War Z*, Jesika Hendricks tells a similar story of community that at first seems like a refuge against the living dead but then falls apart. She and her family have escaped north, where they join others camping on the shore of a lake. At first, "everyone was real friendly," she remembers. "This big, collective vibe of relief. It was kind of like a party at first. There were these big cookouts every night, people all throwing in what they'd hunted or fished, mostly fished." People played instruments or turned on car radios. Everything was communal in those early days of relief; they had found a place of safe haven, far from the cities and, they hoped, the walking dead. "We all sang around the campfires at night, these giant bonfires of logs stacked up on one another."[2]

Then more and more people started showing up, and the resources began to give out. The trees were cut down, the lake was fished clean, and the mood in the camp changed. Jesika describes how "after the first month, when the food started running out, and the days got colder and darker, people started getting mean. There were no more communal fires, no more cookouts and singing. The camp became a mess, nobody picking up their trash anymore." From there, the members of the camp descended into theft and scuffling over the dwindling resources. Jesika's father shot someone trying to break into their van. After their fall into squabbling, the only thing that the group could be united around was resistance against the zombies. Every few days a lone walker would approach, and the campers would gather to kill it. "And then," she says, "we'd all turn on each other again."[3]

Finally, in the long winter, Jesika's parents too are at each other's throats. They have to make hard decisions about staying alive, and they have an epic argument about cannibalizing the dead before Jesika's father acquiesces. Soon, all three of them are surviving off the bodies of their former comrades. The breakdown of community is complete; the members of the camp have begun to consume each other, just like zombies, and the family unit itself has fractured under the strain.

The console/computer game version of *The Walking Dead* differs from many of the other zombie-themed games; here dispatching the undead is not the primary focus of play. Instead, the player's relationships with other characters are privileged, and the story line shifts based on the relationship choices and dialogue that the player chooses while assuming the role of the main character, Lee Everett. Lee rescues an eight-year-old girl, Clementine, shortly after escaping from police custody, and he chooses to be her guardian as they search for her parents and for other survivors. While this community is vital to both of them, other communities they encounter prove to be less functional. In the group of survivors with whom they band, strong disagreements create tensions. Some subunits (for example Kenny, his wife, Katjaa, and his son, "Duck"/Kenny Jr.) are far more interested in taking care of themselves than being a part of the larger group. And other survivors they encounter have less interest in their common survival than in exploiting others.

After leaving Hershel Greene's farm (a location in the comic and TV show as well), the group is holed up at a motel and hungry. They meet some people who live at the St. John's Dairy farm, and they accept the offer to shelter there where there are more resources. However, it quickly becomes apparent that the St. John family has mixed motives for inviting people to their farm; perhaps it's true that they can use some help around the place, but it gradually becomes apparent that they are cannibals feasting on their guests. Sadly, in the ongoing story of *The Walking Dead* as told across various platforms, the breakdown of communities in which characters place their hope is a recurring story. What makes it so heartbreaking each time is that it is clear that these characters need the community, that, like Neville, left alone with these stresses, they will break. They need hope, they need human connection, and in each case they are disappointed.

One of the iconic images from both *The Walking Dead* comic and TV show is the picture of Rick riding a horse down a deserted highway. The opposite lanes of the highway, leaving Atlanta, are jammed with stalled and wrecked vehicles, crammed bumper to bumper. Clearly many wanted to escape the city, although few actually managed to do so. Rick alone is making the slow return; like Neville, he might be the only living person left in the world. He is coming into the city because he is hoping to be reunited with his family. After the solitary trip, he is so anxious for connection that he even tries to engage his horse in conversation. Rescued by Glenn (played by Steven Yeun on the show) after he and his horse are attacked, Rick discovers his family has survived. This is the first of the moments in *The Walking Dead* saga when hope is ignited. As a result of his becoming part of a community, not only do his odds seem to have changed for the better, but the quality of his life seems to be on the upswing. In contrast to the earlier conversation between Rick and Shane about how Rick and his wife were having trouble connecting, now, perhaps because of the extreme circumstances, community and connection become more important and more possible. Sebastian Junger, who has written about the contemporary failures of a sense of community, remarks that "when soldiers experience life in the platoon, or when earthquake survivors experience a brief communal survival effort, everyone's shocked by how good it feels even though the circumstances are horrible. When really it's people re-experiencing their evolutionary origins of being in this small inter-reliant life. And it feels good."[4] So it is for these survivors as well.

With the details differing according to the medium, early in *The Walking Dead* story, Rick's group takes refuge at the Green farm, where Hershel (Scott Wilson on the show) has allowed them to stay while Rick's son Carl (Chandler Riggs on the show) recovers from an accidental shooting. In the comic, Hershel is clear about the boundaries he's establishing ("You folks are welcome to stay here while the boy gets better"), but perhaps Rick and the others hear what they want to hear.[5] Like others in the early stages, this new community seems idyllic. There is food and shelter, and safety from marauding zombies. But the cracks become apparent around the scarcity of resources, among other issues. Within the group itself, Andrea and Allen quarrel over Allen's withdrawal from life since the loss of his wife. Dale confronts Rick's wife, Lori, about her pregnancy, telling her that if the baby is not Rick's, for the good of the group and for Rick's sanity she has to hide the truth.

When the zombies in Hershel's barn escape and kill several of his surviving children, Hershel is distraught and attempts to take his own life before Rick stops him. When Rick later asks him about the possibility of more of them moving into the farmhouse, Hershel is furious. He cites his reasons for wanting them gone. (He has discovered Glenn sleeping with his daughter, he is not going to let strangers move into his dead children's rooms, and Rick's group is, he says, eating through all the food he has stored.) He then orders them off the farm at gunpoint. "Everything went to hell after they came," he explains. "We were doing fine before they got here."[6] What had seemed like a workable community has fallen apart because of zombies, yes, but also because of the tensions that grew out of human relationships. While a functional community could have solved some of these problems, their failure to work together allowed them to become worse.

Because zombie narratives are about survival, they often wrestle with the problem of dwindling resources: What do humans need to survive? What will they do to get those things? Food is the most obvious resource, but other things—weapons, ammunition, transportation, laundry soap, even Twinkies—may be vital to survivors as well. The sisters in *Zombieland*, Wichita and Little Rock (Emma Stone and Abigail Breslin) clearly will do whatever is necessary to keep each other alive, and they admit as much. They steal from and betray Columbus and his traveling partner, Tallahassee (Woody Harrelson), and they are wary about forming any larger community—as wary as Columbus and Tallahassee were, perhaps, when they first meet. Columbus is wheeling his luggage down an interstate packed with wrecked vehicles—very much like that iconic image from *The Walking Dead*—when he hears a vehicle approaching. He sets up a motorcycle as cover and aims his rifle, and Tallahassee pulls up to him in his Cadillac SUV, steps out, and trains a firearm on him in return.

For long seconds they stare at each other, Columbus's hands shaking, Tallahassee's steady. Are these two a threat to each other, or could they possibly work together? At last, when it's clear that something has to happen, Columbus lowers his gun and raises a thumb: "Going my way?" Tallahassee nods. And, amazingly, they are off together, both still alive, and both with a better chance for life because of their encounter.

Human communities and institutions fail during the Zombie Apocalypse, often in spectacular or brutal ways. The human beings inside a place of safety may prove more dangerous than the monsters without, as in Romero's *Day of the Dead*, where scientists and soldiers alike prove to be violent and prone to fatal miscalculations. A place that appears to be a haven may turn out to be a place of betrayal, as the St. John's Dairy Farm in *The Walking Dead* game or the Terminus in the TV show prove to be when it is discovered that their inhabitants are using the people who come to them for food, or when the Manchester blockade in *28 Days Later,* which promises safety for all who arrive there, proves to be a sham. Men who arrive there are killed, while women are set aside to become sex slaves to the soldiers, ostensibly to repopulate the country. Human connection can be dangerous in real life and certainly at the end of the world. Not all Mexican standoffs will end with both parties standing. But all the same, in many zombie narratives, dyads or larger groups try to ride out the Zombie Apocalypse together, seeking not only greater security in numbers, but greater humanity.

The Zombie Guide to Survival treats human connection primarily as a pragmatic asset. ("Whereas a private homeowner may be forced to hold the residence by himself, an apartment building can be defended by all of its tenants"; "Traveling in small groups, as opposed to solo, allows for more secure sleep because individual members can take turns standing watch.")[7] The *Guide* acknowledges the difficulty of assembling a group and keeping them cohesive in a postapocalyptic landscape, where every pressure is magnified and none of the conventional checks on behavior are still present. But although the *Guide* calls getting a group of individuals to cooperate for a long time "the hardest task on earth," it also says the effort is well worth it: "when successful, this group will be capable of anything."[8] Clearly there are more benefits to community than simply another eye or another arm, even to the matter-of-fact narrator of a survival handbook.

SURVIVING AND THRIVING: SEEKING THE GOOD COMMUNITY

Nobody's better off alone.
 —BEN (TYE SHERIDAN), *Scouts Guide to the Zombie Apocalypse*

Sometimes communities in zombie stories come together informally; sometimes they are the last remnants of social institutions, or are institutional reactions to the Zombie Apocalypse. In *The Passage*, Agent Wolgast rescues young Amy from the government installation as virus-vampires break loose to infect the rest of the world, and the two of them create a sort of family. Later in the book, we encounter the First Colony, a formal defensive camp intended to allow humans to survive the infection within high, well-lit fences and governed by a written constitution. As in our own reality, community comes in many forms in stories of the end of the world. But the interaction of human beings in the Zombie Apocalypse works as a sort of laboratory for social understanding. Why do some communities fail while others thrive? What benefits—and detriments—do human beings derive from community? How can we learn something about being connected from these stories that take place after the failure of most communication media (and that thing that keeps many of us connected now, the Internet)? The world of the Zombie Apocalypse has much to teach us about our calling to human connection. So too do many of our wisdom traditions. We will see how the two, in tandem, offer us insight into the nature of community.

In many zombie narratives, groups form around family members. In the various versions of *The Walking Dead*, Rick Grimes first seeks out his wife and son, who headed toward Atlanta and supposed safety; Wichita and Little Rock in *Zombieland* are sisters who form an indivisible unit, and together they will do anything to survive; Harry and Helen gather in the cellar of the abandoned farmhouse around their wounded daughter, Karen, as zombies prowl outside in *Night of the Living Dead*. As in any other disaster, the first impulse in the Zombie Apocalypse seems to be to reach out to the ones we love and those for whom we feel a sense of familial obligation. In *World War Z*, when Philadelphia falls, Gerry Lane (Brad Pitt), his wife, and his daughters escape together in a commandeered Winnebago. They take shelter with another family in Newark as they wait to be evacuated. Surviving leaders of the United Nations want Gerry to lead a task force to investigate this global outbreak. His family is airlifted away, so he can do that work, and taken to a navy vessel where they find the remnants of civilization who are trying to hang on. Aboard that ship in Gerry's absence, they try to re-create some sort of life together.

In *28 Days Later* Frank (Brendan Gleeson) and his daughter, Hannah (Megan Burns), rescue Jim (Cillian Murphy), and together they set out for the Manchester barricade. Frank describes horses playing in a field as "like a family," words we are clearly meant to apply to this new unit. Selena, in fact, retracts her earlier brutal assessment that being alive is as good as it gets in this brave new world. "She's got a dad," she says, "and he's got his daughter." There is something higher, something better, about that connection. As they camp out that night, Jim has a nightmare, and Frank comes over and comforts him, telling him it's just a bad dream. Jim responds groggily, "Thanks, Dad."

The Bennet sisters in *Pride and Prejudice and Zombies* are not only united in the desire to be well wed; they have also trained together in the deadly arts under the tutelage of Shaolin monks. The family that slays together, stays together. When unmentionables pour in through a window at the ball where they first encounter Mr. Bingley and Mr. Darcy, the girls immediately constitute a fighting unit. Their father calls out "Pentagram of Death," and they form a deadly five-pointed star that expands outward as they step further into the room, dismembering zombies with each new movement. The result of their communion is success and safety: "By the time the girls reached the walls of the assembly hall, the last of the unmentionables lay still."[9] The ball is saved, the possibility of romance and marriage continues, and their family remains whole.

In *Shaun of the Dead*, Shaun and Ed rehearse their plans for the Zombie Apocalypse in a series of flash-forwards: kill

Shaun's infected stepfather, rescue Shaun's mum, collect Liz, and hide out in the Winchester until the apocalypse blows over. They too anticipate creating a family unit of sorts, and in reality they end up doing so, although it is a more fragmentary and tentative family than they had planned, and as in many families, not everyone in it gets on. As the plan plays out, Shaun's stepdad, Philip, joins his mum, Ed, and Shaun in Philip's Jaguar, and the car becomes even more crowded when Liz and her flatmates David (Dylan Moran) and Dianne pile in. In fact, there are so many survivors jammed into the car that it erupts into chaos when Philip dies and returns as zombie Philip.

Our first impulse is to create family—even in the Zombie Apocalypse. Thus, a zombie turning on someone she or he had loved in life is among the most horrible moments in any zombie story. For fifty years now, audiences have been thrilled and repulsed by the cellar scenes at the end of *Night of the Living Dead* when we find Karen eating her father and then stabbing her mother to death. As Mark Protosevich said, it was a horrible fall from innocence to imagine that someone could shift from family to predator in the space of moments. What is still repulsive to us in the twenty-first century was flat-out shocking in 1968; *Variety*, the bible of show business, impugned the moral integrity and social responsibility of the filmmakers, the film industry, the exhibitors, and the audience itself, asking about "the moral health of filmgoers who cheerfully opt for this unrelieved orgy of sadism."[10]

In *The Walking Dead* comic, when Hershel's zombie son is among the group of undead that breaks out of the barn and devours his brother and sister, we can understand why Hershel raises the cold barrel of a revolver to his forehead.

Not only is the reality of this attack unbearable, but to be forced to put down the zombie version of a family member is doubly wounding. In *28 Days Later*, Frank's disaster at the Manchester barricade—a drop of blood from a dead zombie drips into his eye, and instantly he knows he is infected—is one of the most traumatic moments of that film, and the violent monster into which he is transformed represents a startling contrast to the gentle and loving father he has been up to that point. *Shaun of the Dead* dramatizes the deaths and revival of Shaun's stepdad and mum, and while the film is a comedy, it still chills us to see these now undead creatures bare their fangs at those they love.

A version of this scene in another medium appears in the first act of the best-selling game *Diablo III*, in which a zombie curse has befallen the thrice-blasted village of New Tristram, and the player is tasked to discover the source of the curse, destroying zombies left and right in the process. (In an affectionate nod to its source material, some of those zombies resemble the corpulent zombie from *Night of the Living Dead*, down to what appears to be a white shirt and tie.) After the player survives some initial combats with zombies of various sorts, Haedrig Eamon, the village blacksmith, asks the player to help him deal with his wife, Mira, who has been infected. He holds out no hope that she can be healed; he wants only for her not to be one of the living dead, profaning his wife's memory with each step. When Haedrig and the player enter the cellar where Mira is quarantined, she transforms, all the while begging her husband to help her, and the player is forced to kill her. It is a shattering scene, but Haedrig proves to be grateful. He would not want a beloved member of his family to suffer that indignity and would have found it hard to end her undead existence on his own.

Comics also offer versions of this ultimate family disintegration. In *Marvel Zombies: Dead Days*, Robert Kirkman
allows us to see the past actions that zombie Spider-Man has
been lamenting through the series: overwhelmed by his supernatural hunger, Peter devours his wife, Mary Jane, and his
Aunt May. When his friend Nova (Richard Rider) flies in the
apartment window to check on them, Peter babbles without
looking up from his meal: "You don't understand—there's
not enough for you—there's not enough.... The hunger—
I had to do this."[11] He then attacks Nova, and even takes a
bite out of his friend Daredevil (Matt Murdock) when he
tries to intervene. Thus do years of superhero team-ups turn
ugly. In later scenes, Nova, Daredevil, and Spider-Man join
other zombie heroes in attacking more of their former friends
and allies and turning them. In other scenes from the *Marvel
Zombies* arc, Hank Pym (Zombie Giant-Man) captures his
uninfected friend the Black Panther and holds him prisoner
so that he can saw off his limbs and devour him a piece at a
time. Pym's zombified wife, Janet, the Wasp, is furious when
she discovers Hank's treachery, although not for the reasons
we might hope. How, she screeches, could he keep such a
sumptuous morsel all to himself?

Scenes from the *Blackest Night* series from DC Comics,
that mythos's version of the Zombie Apocalypse, are similarly unsettling, as friend turns on friend and family member
turns on family member. The Elongated Man, a "B"-level
DC character elevated to prominence in the best-selling
comic event *Identity Crisis*, and his wife kill their friends
and teammates Hawkman and Hawkgirl and turn them into
unliving creatures like themselves. It is disturbing enough
among less iconic figures, but to see the undead versions
of Superman, Aquaman, and Wonder Woman menacing

their Superfriends causes something in us to rebel; it is the antithesis of what we expect from our heroes and heroines. Our most trusted human groupings revolve around family and friends, and if we betray those bonds, what will we not betray?

These scenes from zombie stories, whether played for laughs, tragedy, or gore, horrify us not just because human beings don't do such things to each other (or shouldn't—of course sometimes they do) but because it's unthinkable that members of a family or close friends should turn on each other so violently—friends don't let friends eat friends. Yet we know that in real life, family members and friends often do turn on each other in horrifying ways. Hate and greed are sometimes the currency of relationships that ought to be founded in love. J. Russell notes of the family in *Night of the Living Dead* that the two parents hate each other, and when their daughter becomes a zombie and attacks them both, it's a vivid representation of this hopelessly maimed community.[12] Zombie stories can symbolize our failures to be in healthy communities by taking them to this ultimate breakdown, in which people who have been in relationship attack and feed on each other literally rather than simply metaphorically.

I suggested earlier that our humanity is linked to the call to set aside our own selfish aims, to step out of our self-imposed solipsism, and to seek a larger good. We find this call expressed in wisdom traditions, to be certain, but also in the spiritual understanding of atheists. De Botton notes that "religions seem to know a great deal about our loneliness. Even if we believe very little of what they tell us about the afterlife or the supernatural origins of their doctrines, we can nevertheless admire their understanding of what separates us from strangers and their attempts to melt away one or two of the prejudices that normally prevent us from building connections with others."[13]

That larger good we seek can be lived out most powerfully in healthy families and friendships, and our wisdom teachings tell us that we are at our most human in and because of community. The second of the creation myths in the Book of Genesis tells us that God looks at the solitary human he has created, Adam, and sees that worthy as he is, in his solitude he is incomplete. "It is not good that the man should be alone," God concludes, and he creates a partner and helper to complete him.[14] Having a companion serves a pragmatic purpose (Adam needs Eve to help him accomplish his assigned tasks) but also meets an existential lack (Adam and Eve need each other to achieve their complete humanity). Even though Adam would be in relationship with the Divine and with the other nonhuman creatures of God, it is clear that human community is necessary. Many zombie stories play on the notion of new Adams and Eves who, if they survive, might be able to jump-start the human race. Columbus in *Zombieland* represents such a new Adam—if, admittedly, a neurotic, lonely new Adam—in search of an Eve, and liable to find himself in despair if he doesn't find her, or someone, to break his solitude.

Robert Neville in *I Am Legend* is a tragically lonely character; to be the last of your kind, or to think you are, is among the most tragic fates we can imagine. But even surrounded by others like us we find ourselves lonely in contemporary Western culture. The Hebrew Testament recognizes loneliness as soul-killing. The Psalmist laments that he finds himself alone, without help or company or comfort. It is a condition of deep despair:

How long, O LORD? Will you forget me forever?
How long will you hide your face from me?
How long must I bear pain in my soul,
and have sorrow in my heart all day long?
How long shall my enemy be exalted over me?[15]

People sometimes think of the Psalms as hymns of praise, which some of them are, or as innocuous religious poetry, which they typically are not. Readers are sometimes surprised to discover the bleakness of the Psalms, in which even God seems to have abandoned the speaker. But they have rung true throughout the generations for those who have faced suffering, often in painful solitude like that of Neville:

My God, my God, why have you forsaken me?
Why are you so far from helping me,
from the words of my groaning?
O my God, I cry by day, but you do not answer;
and by night, but find no rest.…
Do not be far from me,
for trouble is near
and there is no one to help.[16]

As Walter Brueggemann notes, the Psalms represent a call for relationship even against the evidence of the moment. They are bold acts of faith that however we might be abandoned by other human beings, God will not abandon us in our desolation.[17] Relationship is possible, even in the midst of despair. There is still, then, hope. As Psalm 25 puts it,

Turn to me and be gracious to me,
for I am lonely and afflicted.

Relieve the troubles of my heart,
    and bring me out of my distress.
Consider my affliction and my trouble,
    and forgive all my sins.

Consider how many are my foes,
    and with what violent hatred they hate me.
O guard my life, and deliver me;
    do not let me be put to shame, for I take refuge
    in you.
May integrity and uprightness preserve me,
    for I wait for you.[18]

To be alone and forgotten is to be spiritually abandoned, but the Psalmists believed that to be in relationship—even a relationship with a God who did not immediately come to their rescue when they called—was clearly preferable to being alone.

It is hope in the face of despair, light in the darkness. When I asked Mark Protosevich what kept Neville going, he used the word "hope," but said it was not about finding a cure for the virus that had transformed his planet. It was the hope that someone else might be out there somewhere, that the rest of his life would not be this soul-killing loneliness.[19]

Still, life together, even with those we love and to whom we are related, is difficult. We know this from our own experience, as well as from the stories we consume. After the creation stories in the Book of Genesis, we find God coming down to set the peoples of the world against each other by taking away their common language. At once, any chance for common endeavor is complicated to the point of social collapse. In the legend of the Tower of Babel (which James L. Kugel regards as an explanation for the fact that Semitic languages are so similar and yet so different), we also find an attempt to explain why, if we were all once related, we have veered so far apart.[20] The early stories of human interaction we find in the Bible tell us that we have always found it hard to live together. In Genesis alone, we read about our common father and mother betraying each other, one brother killing another, a husband offering his wife as a sex slave to gain wealth and power, that same man prepared to offer his son as a human sacrifice, one brother betraying another by stealing his birthright, and one brother almost killed by his other brothers and sold into slavery. Other such outrages multiply throughout the book, which seems in places more like the most shameful reality TV than a record of how we are supposed to live.

Zombie stories are both realistic and hopeful depictions of how human beings live together. Sometimes we see characters transforming in positive ways because of the love and acceptance of others. Selena, when Jim first meets her in *28 Days Later*, is frighteningly cold: "If someone gets infected," she tells him, "you've got between ten and twenty seconds to kill them. It might be your brother or your sister or your oldest friend. It makes no difference." But as she and Jim draw closer, she grows warmer. All four of the damaged main characters of *Zombieland* begin to develop affection for each other. Columbus begins to reach past his fear of relationship to court Wichita. Tallahassee, so traumatized by the loss of his son that he has not yet internalized it, begins to reach out to Little Rock as a surrogate daughter. When we first meet the two sisters, Wichita responds to Columbus's outrage at their betrayal and thievery by saying, "Better you make the mistake of trusting us than us make the mistake of trusting you." But as they travel together and share stories, the sisters begin to reach past their fear and cynicism and start to trust someone else.

Glenn Rhee, in *The Walking Dead* stories, is another clear beneficiary of the power of community. When the zombie outbreak comes, he is a pizza delivery boy so burdened with debt that he fears he would have to get back in touch with his parents and beg them to take him in. But after the dead begin to walk, everything changes. He finds himself falling in with a group that forms outside of Atlanta, and in their presence, he finds new usefulness. His speed, wit, and resourcefulness help to feed the group and offer them small creature comforts that remind them of their humanity. He holds fast to a vision of Rick in his original innocence and calls him to return to his best self. As executive producer David Alpert told *Variety*, while over the course of the show Rick has changed, growing harder and more violent, Glenn has "always embraced the kinder, better Rick, the one who believes in everyone's humanity." From his inauspicious beginnings, Glenn has gone on to become a stalwart member of the group, the "heart of its sprawling cast," and a fan favorite whose hinted-at demise rocks fan boards and threatens to capsize the show.[21] Community has been good for him, and good for us as readers and viewers. As Kirkman notes, Glenn is responsible for almost everything "upbeat or uplifting" that happens on the show, and his relationship with Maggie "is one of the clearest senses of hope that you get from the story."[22]

But often communities seem to fail, and even family members seem more likely to betray each other than call each other to higher and better things. Like the dysfunctional families in Genesis—and our own families, sadly—they turn on each other over resources and over direction. In the original *Dawn of the Dead*, the four protagonists, Fran, Steve,

Roger, and Peter, disagree about the most basic element of the story: holing up in the shopping mall. "This is exactly what we're trying to get away from," Fran protests, but the men are seduced by the goodies and attempt to block off the entrances so that they can keep all of the mall's wonders for themselves. Even though Roger is bitten by zombies, in his delirium he is satisfied with his sacrifice: "We did it, didn't we?... We got it all!" Steve later reacts to the invasion of the bikers indignantly: "It's ours! We took it!" His shouts—and shots—give away their position, and zombies flood into the mall as the humans fight. Ultimately, of course, Fran was right and the men wrong. While she and Peter escape in the helicopter at the movie's end, her poignant question "What have we done to ourselves?" continues to echo. And while the four didn't turn on each other because of their disagreement, two of them are dead and turned to zombies, and the survivors face an uncertain future.

In Romero's *Day of the Dead*, members of the small human community are much more at odds with each other, a return to the visible conflicts of *Night of the Living Dead*. Two groups, scientists and soldiers, are at each other's throats. They argue over who should be in charge and about their relative worth. These verbal conflicts often become physically violent. They threaten each other with guns, physically assault each other, and later begin to kill each other. In the end, as in *Night of the Living Dead*, the disintegration of the community is mirrored when they are overwhelmed by zombies, and we are left to ask—did their failure to work together mean their destruction?

The 2004 remake of *Dawn of the Dead* contains even more commentary on dysfunctional relationships, although it does offer examples of powerful community as well. Early in the film, when Ana (Sarah Polley) is attacked both by the zombie versions of her young neighbor and her boyfriend, we have clear reminders that family and friends can turn on each other. Ana joins a small group of survivors, and as in the original, they seek shelter inside a shopping mall. They are joined by another group, several of whom are infected. While some of the relationships in the movie are healthy and loving, perhaps the most enduring images of the film are of Luda (Inna Korobkina), who dies and then as a zombie gives birth to Andre's (Meki Phifer) "baby." They are discovered by Norma (Jayne Eastwood), who shoots Luda and is herself shot by Andre. Instead of a family bringing new life into the world, we are left with the startling image of Andre, dead, holding his zombie baby. A joyful moment is transmuted into horror; many reviewers remember this scene above all others in the film.

Some of our most ancient as well as modern stories indicate that living together is a challenge. What do they and our wisdom traditions tell us about how we might live in community successfully? Some of the things we learn from observing communities in the Zombie Apocalypse are clearly negative guidelines: *Don't brandish weapons at each other. Don't split up.* So too are many of the guidelines from our wisdom traditions: *Don't kill. Don't steal. Don't covet your neighbor's wife.* In her *Entertainment Weekly* article on the episode "Try" of *The Walking Dead,* Kat Rosenfield finds that Rick is guilty of violating one of the Ten Commandments: "Rick Grimes officially coveted his neighbor's wife so hard that he decided to throw said neighbor out the window".[23] If you want your community to thrive, these might be other things you don't do. But what are the things you *should* do to allow a group to not only survive but flourish?

Zombieland lays down a number of rules, but they are largely about individual survival. Columbus's rules, including "Cardio," "Check Bathrooms," and "Don't Be a Hero," while supremely useful to the lone traveler, don't offer much wisdom about how to be part of a larger group. Tallahassee's rule "No Names," the use of place-names instead of personal names, is his way of keeping people at a distance. The less you know, the less you get hurt. As Columbus says early on, "When you're afraid of everything out there, you quit going out there," and this refers not just to the inhibiting effects of his own shyness and solitude, but to all the ways in which people might put themselves in circulation, as can be seen early on in *Zombieland*.

BUILDING A COMMUNITY WORTH DYING FOR

You are *not* alone.

— RADIO BEACON, *I Am Legend (2007)*

In the early stages of the zombie outbreak, Columbus is visited by his cute neighbor, "405," on whom he's long nursed a crush. She is, it turns out, becoming a zombie; as he observes, "the first girl I let get close tries to eat me." This experience puts in sharp relief his fear of opening himself up to people. How do we live together? Thankfully, some communities actually offer positive rules about that very thing, while wisdom traditions often center on practices that show us how to be better members of communities. Some wisdom actually talks about communities as families, or uses the metaphor of the single body made up of many diverse parts. Christian teachings on the *ecclesia*, the gathering of people brought together around a common goal or purpose, the Buddhist Eightfold Path, and Muslim beliefs about the relationship between religion and community show how spiritual wisdom has been of practical use over the centuries. Some of this wisdom is lived out in communities in our stories; others could clearly benefit from this wisdom.

While community is an important concept in most spiritual traditions, it is essential to Christianity. One of the central mysteries of the Christian faith is that the deity is said to manifest as a trinitarian community, existing in a triangle of never-ending, always-returning love. Jürgen Moltmann writes that "the triune God is community, fellowship, issues an invitation to his community and makes himself the model for a just and livable community in the world of nature and human beings." This is why Moltmann can write that the *ecclesia,* or church, "is the 'lived out' Trinity. In the community, that mutual love is practiced which corresponds to the eternal love of the Trinity."[24] This challenging Christian wisdom suggests that as human beings we are called to form loving communities because we are made in the image of a creator God whose shape is that of a loving community. This is, so to speak, the DNA of the cosmos.

All of the Gospels, the Acts of the Apostles, and the Epistles show us spiritual communities forming around the life and teachings of Jesus, but the Johannine works (the Gospel of John and the three Letters of John) focus especially on the primacy of love for the forming of the *ecclesia* or sacred community. In John's Gospel, we find Jesus saying, "I give you a new commandment, that you love one another. Just as I have loved you, you also should love one another. By this everyone will know that you are my disciples, if you have love for one another."[25] This call to love, which is the sole commandment Jesus gives in John, is so vital that the writer has Jesus repeat it twice in short order:

> This is my commandment, that you love one another as I have loved you.
>
> No one has greater love than this, to lay down one's life for one's friends.
>
> You are my friends if you do what I command you. I do not call you servants any longer, because the servant does not know what the master is doing; but I have called you friends, because I have made known to you everything that I have heard from my Father....
>
> This is my commandment, that you love one another as I have loved you.[26]

All this sounds very much like something Rick says about community early in season 2 of *The Walking Dead*, as he's trying to reach his friend Morgan (Lennie James) on the radio: "There's just a few of us now. So we gotta stick together. Fight for each other. Be willing to lay down our lives for each other if it comes to that. That's the only chance we've got." For Rick, this too is the defining element of real community: the willingness to love so much that you offer your lives for each other.

Love is also the focus of the Johannine letters, which emerged from the early Christian community formed around the Gospel of John. In 1 John, we find the writer saying that what sets the faithful community apart is that they turn away from the violence and jealousy common in the world and embrace the command to love, "for this is the message you have heard from the beginning, that we should love one another." For our context, the passage offers a powerful definition: anyone who does not love is dead already. The walking dead who are dead and the walking dead who are living may be recognized by this simple test: they do not love.[27]

When we talk about love, we can be on slippery ground. Doesn't the Governor in *The Walking Dead* love his daughter so much he can't bear to put her away? Often in our culture when someone says they love us, it means they love their idea of us, their notion of how it is we can make their lives better, more beautiful, more exciting, more complete. When Steve proposes to Fran in the original *Dawn of the Dead*, she rightly turns him down: "It wouldn't be real." Whatever reasons Steve has for proposing, they don't measure up to what love ought to be. Current reality shows like *The Bachelor* and *The Bachelorette*, where we smash people together over a period of weeks and invite them to "fall in love," are manifestations of this combination of physical and emotional attraction that may have more to do with oneself than with the love object. When we try to apply the ideal of love to communities in zombie tales we generally have to move away from easy societal notions about attraction and satisfaction. While we find plenty of sexuality in the apocalypse, true self-giving love can be much harder to locate.

So what should love be? The Greeks recognized *eros*, the passionate love of a lover for the beloved (which we see in Glenn's initial attraction to Maggie on *The Walking Dead*, Columbus's crush on Wichita in *Zombieland*, or the growing attachment between Selena and Jim in *28 Days Later*). They also valued *philios*, the love of a friend for a friend, which is also often displayed in stories of the Zombie Apocalypse. Over the course of *The Walking Dead*, Rick claims both Shane and Daryl as "my brother"; Jon Snow loves both Edd and Sam as brothers on *Game of Thrones*; at the close of *Shaun of the Dead*, both Shaun and Ed overcome their phobia of seeming gay to pronounce their love for each other. *Eros* and *philios* are two powerful manifestations of love, although neither measures up to the highest love possible between humans.

The Greek word for "love" used in John is *agape*, an idea very different from the Western cultural understandings I have been discussing. It is self-giving, sacrificial love, which does not center on what the beloved has to give us in return. When we speak of love as communion with other members of a family or a group, we are not talking about romantic or erotic love, and while friendship may form a vital part of those relationships, like romantic love it remains to a degree dependent on what we offer each other. In our stories and in real life, successful communities are those transformed by agape, the affirming power of the kind of love that Dr. Martin Luther King, Jr., spoke about as "understanding and creative, redemptive goodwill for all men."[28]

In communities where people truly love each other, they put their own needs second and seek to love and serve each other. This is what makes Archie heroic in *Afterlife with Archie*, not bravery or quick-wittedness, although he possesses those qualities as well. But as Veronica tells her father after she and the others have escaped the Halloween dance thanks to Archie's leadership, "behind us, we heard screams coming from the gym, wafting along the night wind... Archie wanted to go back—I could see it in his eyes—to, to help, to do something, anything... but I think it was for me... or maybe it was for Betty... or maybe it was for both of our safety... he didn't, he kept our group pushing forward, kept us running."[29] Archie wants to go back into the scene of horror and rescue more people, but concern for the people he has already rescued, their fears, their safety, takes precedence over even his noble impulse to go to the rescue.

Thus, people in realized communities also discover that they have to forgive each other, because whether families or in all other groups, our willingness to risk sets us up to be hurt. In *Zombieland*, when Wichita opens her heart just a bit and Columbus doesn't immediately make a play for her, she is stung, and when Wichita and Little Rock steal his car—again—Tallahassee is through with them. Selena has closed up like a clam because of the events of *28 Days Later*, and she expects nothing but betrayal, although she secretly hopes for more. Early in *The Walking Dead* series, Daryl initially lashes out at Rick, T-Dog (IronE Singleton), and the others who left his brother Merle handcuffed to the roof, which resulted in Merle's cutting off his hand to escape; it seems a verification of everything Daryl has believed about the world up to that point. What Jon Snow finds most heartbreaking about his betrayal by some members of the Night's Watch is that he was killed not for selfishness; as his vows said, he had renounced the opportunity for fame, land, and honor, even when King Stannis had offered to legitimize him and ennoble him as Jon Stark, Lord of Winterfell and Warden of the North. No, Jon says; I tried to do the right thing, and they murdered me for it. His indignation is proper; like Jesus, to whom the show has made a number of visual references in recounting its story line about a martyr raised from the dead, Jon had put others first, although as often happens, his reward had not been appropriate to his deeds.

Better you make the mistake of trusting us than we make the mistake of trusting you.

Since we are human, and even good humans fail each other, forgiveness is an essential element for life together. In the Gospel of Matthew, Jesus teaches on this characteristic of successful communities in a section scholars sometimes call "The Discourse on Life in the Faithful Community." The Jesus who reveals himself in these passages is a pragmatic leader as well as a lofty spiritual guide, for he offers practical instruction about how a community organized around common goals might succeed. When members fail each other, as they certainly will, he tells them how to deal with those conflicts that threaten to splinter the community: if it is possible, he says, go to the other person and try to resolve the conflict between the two of you, quietly, gently. If that doesn't work, only then should you pull out the big guns and bring in the rest of the community. Approaching each other in this way, rather than immediately seeking to ostracize or shame people, makes reconciliation possible:

> If another member of the church sins against you, go and point out the fault when the two of you are alone. If the member listens to you, you have regained that one.
>
> But if you are not listened to, take one or two others along with you, so that every word may be confirmed by the evidence of two or three witnesses.
>
> If the member refuses to listen to them, tell it to the church; and if the offender refuses to listen even to the church, let such a one be to you as a Gentile and a tax collector.[30]

In pastoral theology classes in seminary we learned about "triangulation," the very human impulse to get someone else to resolve our conflicts with others. In the church, for example, parishioners are always going to the priest or pastor and telling him about some injury, real or imagined, they have received at the hands of a fellow-parishioner. We were taught not to act on these accusations, unless it was to facilitate a meeting between the aggrieved parties. Jesus's teaching puts the onus back on the aggrieved. If in the world of *Shaun of the Dead* Liz has a problem with Ed, she should not talk to Shaun about it, and if Ed has a grievance with Liz, he should not go to Shaun and expect him to work it out. Both should speak directly to the other, involving Shaun or other members of the group only if this direct and private conversation doesn't yield results.

At its conclusion, Jesus's method of dealing with conflict strikes some as calling for the complete expulsion of the offending members. Certainly zombie stories are full of people who are expelled from groups or who think about expelling themselves; consider Merle Dixon, handcuffed by Rick to an Atlanta roof in that early episode of *The Walking Dead*; Daryl, who reacts to the news of his brother's expulsion by inviting the members of his community to go to Hell; or Ving Rhames's Kenneth in the *Dawn of the Dead* remake, who likewise curses his group and considers leaving them. In his reading of the end of this passage, N. T. Wright suggests that it calls for anyone who refuses to be reconciled to his or her *ecclesia* to be treated as an outcast.[31] Still, "outcast" and "outlaw" are different concepts, and it's always important to remember that the "Gentile and the tax collector" Jesus cited as examples might still someday become integral parts of the community.

The Christian Testament contains many instances of Jesus's ministry to Gentiles—non-Jews—and later, under the leadership of the Apostle Paul, Gentiles became the growing edge of Christianity. And as for tax collectors, while they were no more popular in first-century Palestine than agents of the Internal Revenue Service are today, the disciple Matthew,

This statue of Death (ca. 1530), the "Mort Saint-Innocent," originally stood in the Cemetery of the Innocents in Paris, where it was surrounded by a famous fresco of the *Danse Macabre* and human bones. (© Musée du Louvre, Dist. RMN-Grand Palais/Pierre Philibert/Art Resource, NY)

Soldier/artist Percy Delf Smith created this image of "Death Awed" for his series *Dance of Death*, a World War I updating of the medieval Danse Macabre. *Dance of Death: Death Awed*, 1919. Percy John Delf Smith (British, 1882–1948). Etching; The Cleveland Museum of Art, Gift of The Print Club of Cleveland 1922.267.5 (© The Cleveland Museum of Art)

Margaret Bourke-White's 1945 photograph "The Living Dead at Buchenwald" remains one of the most-remembered images of the Holocaust. (Photo by Margaret Bourke-White/ Time Life Pictures/Getty Images)

In George Romero's *Night of the Living Dead* (1968), audiences were chilled by the transformation of Karen (Kyra Schon) from an innocent little girl to a zombie who feasts on her father and kills her mother. (© Image ten/Photofest)

One of the most enduring images from *The Walking Dead*, Rick Grimes (Andrew Lincoln) riding horseback into Atlanta past the wreckage of modern civilization. (© AMC)

Michonne (Danai Gurira) has been transformed by the Zombie Apocalypse on *The Walking Dead* into a fierce warrior, but like all humans, she still needs a community and a higher purpose. (© Gene Page/AMC)

Long a chilling villain on the long-running BBC series *Doctor Who*, in the 2014 episode "Death in Heaven," the Cybermen gained the power to raise the dead as new Cybermen. (© BBC WORLDWIDE LIMITED)

Austin artist Tyler Stout created this *Shaun of the Dead* poster for a special Alamo Drafthouse showing of the film with director Edgar Wright and stars Simon Pegg (Shaun) and Nick Frost (Ed) in attendance. (© Tyler Stout)

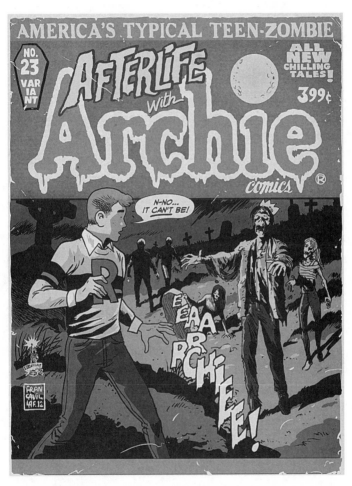

In this variant cover to an issue of *Life with Archie*, artist Francesco Francavilla offered an early vision of the wildly popular *Afterlife with Archie* series to come, a Zombie Apocalypse story set in Riverdale. (© Francesco Francavilla/Archie Comics)

Early in *The Walking Dead* prequel *Fear the Walking Dead*, zombies lurch to the attack. *Fear the Walking Dead* shows how the Zombie Apocalypse unfolds; often, characters awake to discover the world already changed. (© Richard Foreman, Jr./AMC)

The White Walkers, led by the Night's King, are the primary villains on HBO's *Game of Thrones* and have created the undead hordes that menace all the living. As displayed at the International Game of Thrones exhibition in Stockholm on March 11, 2015. (© JONATHAN NACKSTRAND/AFP/Getty Images)

Actor Kit Harington portrays Jon Snow on HBO's *Game of Thrones*. Snow has recognized that the battle between life and death looms larger than any other conflict. (Photo by Astrid Riecken For The Washington Post via Getty Images)

traditional author of the Gospel of Matthew, was thought to have been a tax collector before he became one of Jesus's disciples. Jesus's message seems to be this: with patience, hard work, and forgiveness on both sides, most people can be reconciled and returned to the community, and those on the outside (Gentiles and tax collectors, even) may come into—or return to—the group.

When Jesus calls the members of the *ecclesia* to love and forgive each other, he is not saying "Agree with each other." But he is saying, "These are your people; you need them, they need you, and you will need to learn to get along if you're going to travel together." In the world of the Zombie Apocalypse, as Rick put it, "That's the only chance we've got."

The Apostle Paul writes in his Letter to the Romans that the members of a community may differ radically from each other but that they all have something to offer each other:

> For by the grace given to me I say to everyone among you not to think of yourself more highly than you ought to think, but to think with sober judgment, each according to the measure of faith that God has assigned.
>
> For as in one body we have many members, and not all the members have the same function, so we, who are many, are one body in Christ, and individually we are members one of another.
>
> We have gifts that differ according to the grace given to us: prophecy, in proportion to faith; ministry, in ministering; the teacher, in teaching; the exhorter, in exhortation; the giver, in generosity; the leader, in diligence; the compassionate, in cheerfulness.
>
> Let love be genuine; hate what is evil, hold fast to what is good; love one another with mutual affection; outdo one another in showing honor.[32]

In Rick's community in *The Walking Dead*, we find members with many gifts. Some have a gift for battle. Rick has the gift—and the curse—of leadership. Michonne is a warrior, a zombie-killing machine who helps keep the community safer. Carol has the gift of making hard decisions. Daryl has the gift of discernment; he can tell whether someone is trustworthy or not. When Rowan Williams writes about Paul's emphasis on the importance of everyone in the community—the metaphor of a single body, as opposed to a loose conglomeration of parts—he recognizes the interconnection of those in a successful community. It's not just, as a utilitarian explanation might have it, that everyone has his or her part to play, but that everyone has his or her gift to give. "Each of us," Williams says, "has something the other desperately needs—so that our attitude to one another is not only welcome or service, but also grateful dependence."[33]

We can see this acted out powerfully in the tradition of the Desert Mothers and Fathers. Like the Zombie Apocalypse, this early branch of the Christian tradition offers us a laboratory for human interaction. Many of these eccentric hermits went to the desert because they felt that the world was falling apart. But what they discovered, even in their protoapocalyptic times, men and women alike, was that they too were called to be in community as well to escape. Abba (Father) Antony, whom we know now as St. Anthony, stated the grounding wisdom of the tradition when he proclaimed, "Our salvation is with our brother."[34] Without our brother and sister, we will never become what we are called to be— and we will never live into our own highest callings. But as Jesus noted, to do the hard work of community means we need to find ways to remain together and work out our differences, and that requires a commitment to the community itself. Amma (Mother) Syncletica spoke about the damage that is done to both individuals and faith communities when people are constantly packing up and moving on. She asks: How can you learn to be yourself in Christ unless you spend concentrated time in a community of people trying to live into their own understandings of what they are called to?

Finally, the Desert also tells us that forgiveness is essential, both forgiveness of ourselves and of others. Many of the stories passed on by the tradition are about unwillingness to judge others even for things about which we might judge ourselves. When a priest ordered a brother to leave the gathering because of his sins, Abba Bessarion got up and accompanied the miscreant, telling the assembled brothers, "I, too, am a sinner." Abba Moses, a reformed highwayman, was invited to sit in judgment on a brother who had sinned. At first he refused, but when the gathering insisted, he put together a little object lesson for them: he took an old leaky basket, filled it with sand, and put it on his back. When the brothers came out to meet him, naturally they were confused, and they asked him, "What does this mean, Abba? What are you doing?"

He told them, "My sins run out behind me and I do not see them, and yet you ask me to come today and judge another."

The story ends with them getting the message: they did not condemn the brother who had sinned but forgave him and accepted him back into their fellowship.

Of course it may be easier to forgive when our lives are not on the line, and the stories of the Zombie Apocalypse contain examples of communities who are too forgiving when, for their own safety, it would be better to expel someone. Merle was a loose cannon who endangered everyone else; the wise decision might have been to expel him and never look back. I explore this sort of decision-making and the grounds behind it in chapter 3. But forgiveness will never be easy; in the Discourse on Life in the Faithful Community, Jesus responds to Peter's question about how often we should forgive others by essentially saying, "Forever." If famously difficult types like the Desert Fathers and Mothers could learn to live together, that bodes well for all of us. Learning to disagree well and learning to forgive each other are valuable traits in everyday life, and are that much more necessary in the Zombie Apocalypse.

Of course, it can be hard to have thoughtful conversations when you are on the run for your life, and there may not be an opportunity to reconcile with someone when they may become a zombie in ten or twenty seconds—or in a day or two. Although Jesus did not have the Zombie Apocalypse in mind when he offered his discourse to his followers, it might be useful to have some ground rules in place from the start to help guide people toward healthy relationship, and here is where our wisdom traditions have excelled at providing practical guidance.

Two branches of the Christian tradition, the Benedictine and the Augustinian, offer tangible rules for how people ought to live in community. Augustine of Hippo was powerfully interested in friendship: most of the important incidents in his autobiography take place with a friend or relation present, and he thought of friendship as being essential not just to his emotional but to his spiritual well-being. The short Rule attributed to Augustine has very practical guidelines. It begins thusly: "The main purpose for you having come together is to live harmoniously in your house, intent upon God in oneness of mind and heart."[35] Although we might imagine the monastics gathered under this Rule to be trying to hide out from the outside world, in ways that perhaps resemble many of the groups in our zombie narratives, hiding out in houses, compounds, shopping malls, and pubs, this call is to do more than simply hide and protect oneself. As Augustinian scholar Thomas F. Martin observes, this early passage tells us that this "oneness" was "not only inward looking but equally outward reaching...neither closed off nor narrowly self-protecting."[36] It suggests to us that the pragmatic rules of *Zombieland*, as useful as they may be in helping an individual like Columbus stay one step ahead of the zombie horde, cannot be considered definitive when humans join into communities, which is another set of difficulties. Indeed, this is what Tallahassee communicates to Columbus early in their collective life together: "Here's the deal: I'm not easy to get along with, and I'm sensing you're a bit of a bitch." Columbus's rules make him more difficult, not more safe, in community.

As in other wisdom traditions, Augustine's Rule teaches that a community has a unified focus, a purpose (hence our calling such a community an *ecclesia*, a Greek word referring to a community bound together by common goals and values). In the world of the Zombie Apocalypse those goals may be unstated, and probably are. They probably lean more toward common defense and gathering of resources than common prayer, for example, but the monastic rules also lean toward practical questions. Early on, Augustine drew from the life of the early Christian church in saying "Call nothing your own, but let everything be yours in common. Food and clothing shall be distributed to each of you by your superior, not equally to all, for all do not enjoy equal health, but rather according to each one's need."[37] Rather than hoarding privately, the brothers or sisters living under the rule are enjoined to offer up their resources for the common good, to seek forgiveness and ask pardon, and to respect their leaders. Leaders, for their part, are asked to think of themselves not as superior (although they may be in authority and in gifts) but as servants:

> The superior, for his part, must not think himself fortunate in his exercise of authority but in his role as one serving you in love. In your eyes he shall hold the first place among you by the dignity of his office, but in fear before God he shall be as the least among you. He must show himself as an example of good works toward all. *Let him admonish the unruly, cheer the fainthearted, support the weak, and be patient toward all* (1 Thes 5:14). Let him uphold discipline while instilling fear. And though both are necessary, he should strive to be loved by you rather than feared, ever mindful that he must give an account of you to God.[38]

These words assume some resonance when we think about leaders in our stories. In *The Walking Dead*, for example, how do they apply to Rick, who goes from naïve deputy to ruthless leader? What do they suggest about the Governor? What would an ideal leader look like?

Significantly, Augustine is remembered in Christian circles as the popularizer of the doctrine of original sin, the concept that all of humanity is fallen because of the original sin of Adam and thus tends toward the wrong desires and impulses. While this is perhaps a bit reductive—Augustine was also a great believer in the power of beauty and truth to impel us toward the Divine—what is most important for us may be that even in someone who acknowledged the pain and difficulties that sometimes come from being human, Augustine affirmed the power of human relationship. In the

Zombie Apocalypse, often we see the worst rather than the best of people; when people make decisions out of fear, scarcity, and self-interest, it rarely translates into humans' most enlightened behavior. But rather than run from the faults and failures of the human, Augustine encouraged us to be present to others, to interact with others, and to love and to serve others, with all the dangers that might entail. In the film *World War Z*, Gerry is on the one hand working to build a better world for his family, left behind on the ship. On the other hand they are safe, and he could remain there with them. Rather than cocooning himself with his family, he crisscrosses the globe, working with people from Asia to the Middle East to Europe to better the conditions of all. He serves. He is an example of good works to all. He is, as his former work with the United Nations suggests, a citizen of a larger world.

Donald X. Burt has written that Augustine saw "that the great tragedy of the human condition was alienation." But if, in fact, alienation is our great tragedy, he believed that "love is the glue by which the divisions inside and outside of us can be corrected."[39] In loving and serving each other—whatever that might look like to you—we are realizing our best selves. Agent Wolker in *The Passage* becomes his best self when he rescues the girl Amy, making her welfare more important than his FBI assignment. Shaun begins to become his best self when he resolves to get up off his couch and gather those he loves in a place of safety. And Columbus becomes his best self when he revises his rules for individual survival from "Don't Be a Hero" to "Be a Hero" in order to rescue other members of his community, whatever the risk to himself. Although it is countercultural wisdom in the radically individual West, we need each other, and sometimes being in community may be all that stands between us and despair.

Some years ago, I heard Archbishop Desmond Tutu speaking about the African concept of Ubuntu at the National Cathedral in Washington, D.C. Ubuntu, Tutu explained, is the notion that "a person is a person through other persons. It is not, 'I think, therefore I am.' It is rather, 'I am human because I belong. I participate. I share.'" What Dean Samuel Lloyd concluded about their conversation that day was that Ubuntu might actually be the most basic element of Christian practice: "We need each other. I can't be me without you. That is the heart of what Christians mean by being the body of Christ, the church."[40]

At the end of *Zombieland*, after Columbus has traveled across country with three difficult and sometimes contentious others, the movie's closing scene offers a bookend to its opening ("See that guy there?"). In it, he looks at Tallahassee, Wichita, and Little Rock, and he says:

> That's me realizing that those smart girls in that big, black truck and that big guy in that snakeskin jacket—they were the closest to something I'd always wanted but never really had: a family.
>
> I trusted them and they trusted me....
> We had hope.
> We had each other.
> And without other people...
> Well, you might as well be a zombie.

Community in the Zombie Apocalypse is not just about survival; it's about humanity. It's about living up to the best that is in us. Many zombie stories end badly; at their very best, most of the world we knew is gone. But there is still an antidote to the soul-killing curse of solitude and alienation, and that is each other. Joined by the bonds of love—not just by pragmatism—we are called (and can call each other) to a higher standard. As Rowan Williams wrote, in such a body, we are offered something superior to the simple utility we have for each other.

That love, as I have shown, sometimes calls us to give all we have for our communities. In many of our stories of the Zombie Apocalypse, favorite characters (like Frank in *28 Days Later*, Sergeant Doyle [Jeremy Renner] in *28 Weeks Later*, Dale and Hershel in *The Walking Dead*, and of course Robert Neville in *I Am Legend*) do not survive, but they have lived with a sort of integrity, and die with the knowledge that they have done what they should. Sometimes you do the right thing—even though it costs you everything. In chapter 3, we'll explore what it means to do the right thing, how we know what that thing is, and what we do when we aren't sure what the right thing might be. Exploring the ethics of the Zombie Apocalypse, like our other explorations, will lead us back to our own lives, so that we can understand why, out of the wide range of human behavior, even in times of chaos, we might say that some things are right and some things are wrong.

CARRYING THE FIRE

The Ethics of the Zombie Apocalypse

The monsters that rose from the dead, they are nothing compared to the ones we carry in our hearts.
— ADMIRAL XU ZHICAI, MAX BROOKS, *World War Z*

Beware that when fighting monsters, you do not become a monster. For when you gaze long into the Abyss, the Abyss is gazing back at you.

— FRIEDRICH NIETZSCHE, *Beyond Good and Evil*

MONSTERS WALK THE EARTH: EVERYTHING IS PERMITTED

IN CORMAC McCARTHY'S PULITZER PRIZE–winning novel *The Road*, the main characters are a father and son who try to survive in a postapocalyptic world where they are perpetually hungry, perpetually cold, and in danger, every moment of every day. Early in the story, they flee some men driving a ramshackle truck somehow still miraculously supplied with diesel. One of those men later stumbles into their camp, and as he talks to the man, he looks at the boy in a way his father mislikes, almost, one might think, as if he were sizing him up for a meal. The confrontation turns violent, and the stranger grabs the boy and puts a knife to his throat; the man puts a bullet through the stranger's forehead, and father and son flee for their own lives. When they eventually return to their old campsite, they find that the stranger's corpse has been boiled and eaten by his comrades; nothing remains but his skin, bones, and innards.

Afterward, when they can reflect a bit, the man and the boy have this conversation:

> You wanted to know what the bad guys looked like. Now you know. It may happen again....
>
> He sat there cowled in the blanket. After awhile he looked up. Are we still the good guys?
>
> Yes. We're still the good guys.
>
> And we always will be?
>
> Yes. We always will be.
>
> Okay.[1]

With the breakdown of society, the old rules are gone, the old institutions have disappeared, and the old ways of knowing who is good and who is bad have gone with them. The church, the law, the government, all those things that used to provide guardrails for human behavior have vanished, and the survivors are left to make their way in a world where not everyone lives up to old ways of thinking and doing. In this chapter I am using the story of the Zombie Apocalypse to explore human ethics and to shine light on our own post-9/11 reality. Sadly, even though no zombies walk our earth, these stories are so popular with us because they reflect some of the ways we have reacted to our own perceived menaces.

The Zombie Survival Guide explains the changes that come with the Zombie Apocalypse this way: "When the living dead triumph, the world degenerates into utter chaos.

All social order evaporates. Those in power, along with their families and associates, hole up in bunkers and secure areas around the country.... With the total collapse of law and order, small bands of individuals emerge to assert their authority. Looters, bandits, and common thugs prey on the survivors, taking what they want and indulging in whatever pleasure they can find."[2] Instead of law and one rule for all, people begin to make their own rules; those rules vary wildly across the human family in the face of mortal terror and threat.

The man and the boy struggle to hold onto old moralities represented by those rules and codes I discussed in chapter 2; they still cling to commandments, like "Thou shalt not kill," that echo from the old world into their new reality. They talk often about how they are "carrying the fire," and it seems clear that although they do not articulate what that means, in some way they are holy bearers of something important and noble that the world still needs. "Carrying the fire" or, we might say, "doing the right thing," is one of the main things that keeps them moving, step by painful step, through a world fallen apart. Otherwise it would be easy to give up, perhaps to choose the easy way of suicide that the man's wife, the boy's mother, took before the story began.

Rick Grimes begins *The Walking Dead* as a maintainer of the old ways; when he launches himself full bore into the chaos of the Zombie Apocalypse, after all, it is as a deputy, complete with uniform, hat, and gun. When Rick and his family are reunited outside Atlanta, he has just killed his first few zombies. He is struggling to reconcile the act of shooting something so human-looking with his self-image as a man reluctant to use force, reluctant to draw his gun. On TV, the shootout in which he is first wounded is emblematic—Rick's colleagues, including Shane, start shooting when the first suspect comes out of the car, gun blazing, but Rick still calls out a warning: "Put it down! Put the gun down!" His regard for the sanctity of human life persists for a while. In the season 1 episode "Wildfire," Rick tells Daryl emphatically, "We don't shoot the living." But as he traverses his long arc, Rick begins to become more pragmatic about the use of violence— much more like Shane, many commentators note, who is willing to resort to any number of ethical shortcuts to protect those about whom he cares.

In this brave new world that has such people (and monsters) in it, how much is too much? How far too far? Early on, Rick tries to hold onto old values, but he soon discovers that it can be hard even to know—let alone do—what is right. In the season 2 episode "Bloodletting," Rick reenters a church he and his crew have cleared of walkers. He approaches an image of the crucified Jesus hanging over the altar, and although he says he is not a religious man, he prays for guidance, for "some indication that I'm doing the right thing. You don't know how hard that is to know. Well . . . maybe you do."

Some wrestle with how to adapt old rules to a new world. Others, however, have taken the fall as liberation, and there is precedent for this as well. The founder of the Order of the Assassins, Hassan i Sabbah, purportedly said as he died: "Nothing is true, everything is permitted." As Friedrich Nietzsche said, the Death of God opens all possibilities, and some survivors take their new freedom from regulation as far as it can be taken; they kill, torture, maim, enslave, and eat, all as they please. *The Zombie Survival Guide* notes that we may not know what the brigands of the Zombie Apocalypse will look like, how they will travel, or how they will be armed, but "what is certain is that they will always be on the lookout for loot. As time goes by, this might mean women. Later, it could mean children for slavery or new warriors," and eventually "these ruffians could look to their fellow humans as a last-ditch source of food."[3]

This transformation of humans into monsters is illustrated time and again in our stories. In *Day of the Dead*, Captain Rhodes (Joe Sabato) has threatened Sarah (Lori Cardille) with both rape and execution. She says of him, "He can't be that inhuman."

No, John (Terry Alexander) responds, "he's human. That's what scares me."

Late in *The Road*, the man and the boy hide and watch a caravan of horror roll past, as grotesque as something out of a Mad Max film or a painting by Hieronymus Bosch: masters with their slaves, male and female, trailing behind to be used for sex or food or whatever their masters will.

Ethics is the branch of inquiry devoted to exploring questions about how we live and about what is good; hence the boy's question "Are we the good guys?" is a question about ethics. In a world where people have unlimited freedom to choose their own behavior, we should expect that more people will descend into the abyss. As Kim Paffenroth writes, the scientist Logan (David Liberty) in *Day of the Dead* (in his own way, the soldier Captain Rhodes's monstrous equal) understands ethics not as a set of behaviors to aspire to but as a rigged game one is tricked into, following the promise of some sort of reward. "Anyone who saw ethics as this kind of comical charade would seek to maximize the amount he 'tricked' others and minimize the amount that he himself would be 'tricked' into doing silly good deeds."[4] Under the "old" ethics, characters like Logan or Rhodes might feel constrained from doing what they really want.

It should not surprise us then to see people going off the rails in this world without ethical checks. After all, even in our present world, where standards for individual, group, and national behavior exist and aberrant actions have consequences, some individuals still choose mass murder or serial rape, some groups unleash suicide bombers, some nations elect to export terror or invade their neighbors. Although we have many rules about what cannot and should not be done, it can still sometimes be hard to determine whether we are the good guys. It remains somewhat easier to identify the bad guys. As the man teaches the boy throughout *The Road*, the bad guys are those who use others, who attempt to control others, who kill others, who consume others, whether metaphorically or literally. No matter what the extremity, these two will not descend to that, will never become monsters:

> We wouldn't ever eat anybody, would we?
> No. Of course not.
> Even if we were starving?
> We're starving now.
> You said we weren't.
> I said we weren't dying. I didn't say we weren't starving.
> But we wouldn't.
> No. We wouldn't.
> No matter what.
> No. No matter what.
> Because we're the good guys.
> Yes.
> And we're carrying the fire.
> And we're carrying the fire. Yes.
> Okay.[5]

In *The Road*, as in many stories of the Zombie Apocalypse, people appear at their most monstrous when they most resemble zombies; the consumption of human flesh is one of our greatest taboos. Those who do it—particularly those who eat others regularly or even systematically—are held up as particularly loathsome. Thus our horror at discovering the secrets of Terminus in *The Walking Dead* series and the dairy farm in *The Walking Dead* game, or of Jesika Hendrick's account in *World War Z* of the degeneration of her northern camp into cannibalism. During the course of their conversation, Jesika's interviewer kneels to examine a pile of bones, all broken, the marrow extracted. "She holds up what looks like a miniature femur. It has been scraped clean by a knife."[6] Not even children were immune from this exploitation and desecration, not even infants. And these cannibals Jessika described were not murderers, rapists, power-mad autocrats; they were simply people like her parents, frightened, hungry, willing to violate this great taboo to stay alive.

In *The Road*, we as readers and filmgoers are exposed to these horrors of the apocalypse when the man and the boy enter a house and find a locked trapdoor in a pantry. They are starving, and despite their trepidation, the man knows that they must find food. They descend the stairs by the light of the man's lighter, and what they find down there is a vision of Hell:

> Huddled against the back wall were naked people, male and female, all trying to hide, shielding their faces with their hands. On the mattress lay a man with his legs gone to the hip and the stumps of them blackened and burnt. The smell was hideous.
>
> Jesus, he whispered.

> Then one by one they turned and blinked in the pitiful light. Help us, they whispered. Please help us.[7]

The man drops the lighter in his panic. He and the boy run out the front door of the house—just as four men and two women come into sight, returning to their larder. The father and son barely escape the fate of those in the cellar (and of all those these human ghouls capture), of keeping their captors alive for another day, another week, another month by giving up their own flesh.

In his introduction to *The Walking Dead* graphic novel, Robert Kirkman noted that in his story, as in most Zombie Apocalypse stories, the human drama comes not from the confrontations with zombies, who so vastly outnumber the living, but from the behavior of the human beings. After the failure of human institutions, of our police and justice systems, of our armed forces, survivors are left to create their own institutions and to rediscover or reject the importance of personal ethics. Even good people, Kirkman said in an interview on season 5 of the TV show, can find themselves making damaging ethical choices in the name of survival. "These are characters that have evolved into something that is probably unrecognizable to them.... They're slowly realizing that in order to survive in this world they have to be monsters."[8]

In this section, we want to explore the extremes of human behavior, the villainy into which some people descend when checks are removed and their personal survival becomes their foremost value. If ethics is about the questions "What is the good life?" and "What is the right thing to do in a given situation?" then "Survival" or "Survive" are perfectly valid answers. But how to survive? For some characters in these stories, the way to survive is to wield power over others, to exercise it, to do whatever is necessary to keep themselves or their communities alive. Not surprisingly, in most such cases we are talking about the villains of our stories—about the cannibal inhabitants of the farmhouse in *The Road*, about the Governor, Negan, and other tyrants in *The Walking Dead*, about Major West (Christopher Eccleston) and his soldiers in *28 Days Later*. Angela Kang told me onstage that the dramatic core of *The Walking Dead* series is simply that in their story, "The monsters are not the zombies. They're the human beings."[9] So as I explore the ethics of the Zombie Apocalypse, I'll consider what some people are willing to do to survive, and what those actions may cost them in terms of their humanity, beginning with the human monsters who make the choices most of us would call least ethical.

Ramsay Bolton (Iwan Rheon), born the bastard son of Roose Bolton in the Song of Ice and Fire/*Game of Thrones* saga and raised to legitimacy and rule, was recently named the most hated character on TV by the *New York Times*.[10] Ramsay's incessant employment of rape, torture, flaying, and execution to take advantage of the chaos in the *Game of Thrones* world certainly qualifies him for this dubious honor, but critic Myles McNutt suggests that his use of such terrorizing tactics is a strategy as much as a moral failing. Ramsay's victims do his bidding and further his goals; Reek/Theon (Alfie Allen) completely submerges himself and his personality to avoid further pain and disfigurement at Ramsay's hands, and Theon tells those like Sansa Stark (Sophie Turner) who fall into Ramsay's clutches that if they don't do what Ramsay says, there is much worse in store for them.

McNutt, analyzing the season 6 *Game of Thrones* episode "Home," in which Ramsay kills his father, stepmother, and infant brother to gain complete control of the North, writes that Ramsay is "*choosing* to ignore a sense of morality that could exist because he believes it to be the path to power."[11] Ramsay believes he is furthering his ambitions by putting away conventional notions of morality and ethics—by tamping down what makes us human and humane, in other words. This may be even more monstrous—the idea that he is consciously choosing to be monstrous in order to consolidate his power.

Stannis Baratheon (Stephen Dillane), who had carved out a rigid but honorable place in the hearts of *Game of Thrones* audiences, represents a sad counterpart to Ramsay Bolton's story of ambition. Stannis initially seems to be a person of great integrity and high moral fiber. In the wake of his conversion to the worship of the Lord of Light, however, and because he is convinced that he alone can rally the kingdom against the coming zombie hordes, he makes a series of morally dubious decisions intended to consolidate his rule, most notably consigning his daughter to the flames as a sacrifice to the Lord of Light so that his army can win a great victory. Ramsay Bolton received his comeuppance at the hands of his former victim Sansa Stark, in the season 6 episode "Battle of the Bastards," but Stannis's fate, on TV, at least, was sealed a year earlier. "King Stannis" compromised his ethical standards in the hope of protecting himself and the Realm from the White Walkers and their undead army, and it cost him everything. Like Roose, his call to power also turns him into a monster, if one who does evil out of the best motivations.

The will to power motivates many of the villains in the Zombie Apocalypse. They believe that by exercising power ruthlessly, they are giving themselves and those who follow them the best possible chance for survival. Never mind that for those of us sitting out the Zombie Apocalypse their actions seem sociopathic or even insane; as I've mentioned, even Rick Grimes can say "We know what needs to be done and we do it." If such a moral exemplar can wind up—at least for a time—at this place of moral pragmatism, should it surprise us that the villains we encounter are so reprehensible when survival is at stake?

If everything is permitted and the old rules have vanished, what makes men and women monsters in the Zombie Apocalypse? Sometimes, interestingly, storytellers make characters into literal monsters. In the *Marvel Zombies* tales, we are given the appalling vision of some of our greatest pop culture heroes as flesh-eating zombies who, despite their consciousness, continue to eat others in order to survive. In *30 Days of Night*, Eben ((Josh Hartnett in the film) sheds his humanity, becomes an undead killing machine to fight the vampires invading his town, and, at last has to kill himself so that he will not be a danger to those he loves. In *New Deadwardians*, to combat the zombie plague of "The Restless," many aristocrats make a similar supreme sacrifice and take "the Cure." They become vampires so that they can roll back the zombie tide. As "The Young," they do not set off whatever sensors motivate the Restless to feed, and they become unstoppable, unkillable soldiers in the service of queen and empire.

As with Eben, however, this transformation comes at a cost. Chief Inspector George Suttle, the central character of the graphic novel, walks up to a fence, beyond which stands a zombie horde, and reflects that "the Restless do not heed me. As one of the Young, I am as a blank to them. Yet we are so alike in our lifeless lives. I am eternal and sentient. They are enduring and mindless. But otherwise, we are all equally dead."[12] The graphic novel follows Inspector Suttle as he seeks to reclaim something life-giving in his never-ending life, but many of his fellow Young never find it. They are locked into forever without anything to give them pleasure except, perhaps, the Tendencies that some of them develop for blood and human flesh.

Although they are not literal zombies, the Quislings in the book *World War Z* are the closest thing to it. Joe Muhammad describes Quislings as "the people that went nutballs and started acting like zombies." In this war, as Joe points out, people couldn't raise their hands and surrender; zombies don't know the difference between fleeing meat, fighting meat, and surrendering meat. Some people, he concludes, couldn't accept that they didn't have that traditional out, surrender. "It put them right over the edge. They started moving like zombies, sounding like them, even attacking and trying to eat other people." Joe and his squad discovered their first quisling when it attacked one of them—and bled when shot, which, of course, zombies cannot do, having no functional circulatory system. But although they had physical weaknesses true zombies don't have—Quislings were susceptible to cold, to hunger, to mortal damage other than to the brain—like zombies, they wouldn't stop, and like zombies, they couldn't be reasoned with. "There was nothing left to talk to. These people were zombies, maybe not physically, but mentally you couldn't tell the difference."[13]

These men and women chose not to fight their monsters; instead, they gave in to them, went over to their side. In the battle between Life and Death, they chose Death. In all these cases, characters literally become monsters in response to the onslaught of monsters. In most of our stories, however, villains, while monstrous, are still definably human, which may make them even more menacing.

The Harry Potter novels and films contain little in the way of zombies (if much about apocalypse), but I've previously written on Harry Potter and the so-called Unforgivable Curses, and that analysis turns out to be germane to our discussion about ethics and what makes for monstrous human beings.[14] What these three most-reviled magic spells have in common is that each of them is about exercising control over another human being. The Imperius Curse allows a wizard to control the actions of others, taking away their agency and free will. The Cruciatus Curse tortures others, causing them suffering and either inducing them to do the torturer's bidding or to suffer at the torturer's whim. Lastly, the Avada Kadavra, the Killing Curse, represents the ultimate abuse of power, the ability to instantly impose death on another person. That these spells are considered "unforgivable" illuminates the ethical dimension of J. K. Rowling's world; because they allow someone to exercise ultimate control over another, these curses must be shunned, and anyone who employs them must be punished by banishment and imprisonment.

In the zombie tales, we discover characters who similarly control the actions of others, killing them, torturing them, restricting their movement, and forcing them to do what they would not choose to do of their own volition. The "bad guys" in *The Road,* who kidnap survivors, lock them away, and eat them, are obvious examples. In *28 Days Later,* Major Hill chains up one of his infected men, but he also imprisons Sergeant Ferrell (Stuart McQuarrie), who refuses to participate in the Major's plan to kill or rape the survivors who arrive at the barricade. We find characters in these stories torturing others, often simply for their own amusement, or to confirm their power. At the close of season 6 of *The Walking Dead,* Negan stalks among the members of Rick's band brandishing his trusty baseball bat, Lucille, torturing them (and viewers) with the knowledge that he is getting ready to kill one of them.

In the season 3 episode "When the Dead Come Knocking," the Governor interrogates Glenn and Maggie using threats and humiliation, and later in the season, he orders brothers Merle and Daryl to fight to the death as a way to prove Merle's loyalty. And, of course, in story after story, we find characters like these killing other living humans, despite our long-standing restrictions against doing so, sometimes without even the justification that it is for their own survival. These monsters, like zombies, kill because they can, because it is their nature. But unlike zombies, some of them kill because they enjoy it.

In our own legal and ethical systems, we might imagine similar objections to the kinds of abuses enabled by the Unforgiveable Curses, but these have been complicated by our responses to the 9/11 terror attacks, a crisis that has shaped our own lives. Over the last fifteen years, in America and, to a lesser extent, Britain, strong leaders have assumed powers they had not previously held. They have authorized actions that in peacetime would have been considered at best excessive and at worst criminal. The practice of rendition (kidnapping of foreign nationals and transferring them to places on allied soil where they can be interrogated and incarcerated) and of torture (whether by allied nations or by the Central Intelligence Agency) are clear violations of the Geneva Conventions, ethical rules that civilized nations have set up to guide how war and combat are to be conducted. In the face of what some called a threat to our survival, these rules created for the very purpose of limiting our inhumanity to our foes were ignored.

Even in times of high stress and imminent danger, some argue that ethical standards matter. Perhaps they matter even more when we face the choice of abandoning them. Comic book heroes and heroines typically adhere to an absolute code prohibiting them from taking the life of another. In *The Dark Knight*, the Joker (Heath Ledger) knows that this is the "one rule" Batman (Christian Bale) follows, although the Joker believes it to be Batman's great weakness instead of his great strength. In Marvel Comics, almost all the heroes have a conviction not to kill, even in the face of the apocalypse—which the world so often seems to be facing in comics and comic adaptations. In the comic *Uncanny Avengers*, the Wasp (clearly not the Wasp of Zombie Avengers) is asked whether she has ever used lethal force: "Never. Avengers don't kill. If we cast aside our principal beliefs when the chips are down, what does that say about us?"[15] Early on, Rick Grimes says, "We don't shoot living beings." Later, however, he changes his refrain. When he encounters new survivors, he asks them: "How many zombies have you killed? How many living beings have you killed? Why?" The answers matter. Rick has come to accept that sometimes one must kill living beings, but it must be for sufficient reason. They must pose a threat to individuals or to the group.

Is it possible that you can do something immoral (or immoral in normal times) for a good reason? Can you do something monstrous in service of a greater good? And if you do, does that make you better or worse than the monsters you oppose?

In Christian doctrine, humans are understood to be fallen. How exactly we are fallen and redeemed is a matter of some theological debate, but there is perhaps general agreement that what this means practically is that, left to our own devices, humans will tend to choose bad over good. Original sin—the belief that because Adam sinned, he passed this "sin gene" down to the rest of the human race—is a way of thinking about human nature. Some find it depressing; others consider it realistic. Augustine formulated the doctrine of original sin in response to the Celtic theologian Pelagius, who believed that because they are made in the image of God, humans have the ability to lead spotless lives through their own power. For Pelagius, human beings have the power in and of themselves to choose good over evil.

As encouraging as I find Pelagius's arguments, I also see the merit in Augustine's, and in the Apostle Paul's recognition that as human beings, we often make poor choices even when we know the good. Paul articulated this beautifully in his Letter to the Romans:

> For we know that the law is spiritual; but I am of the flesh, sold into slavery under sin.
>
> I do not understand my own actions. For I do not do what I want, but I do the very thing I hate.
>
> Now if I do what I do not want, I agree that the law is good.
>
> But in fact it is no longer I that do it, but sin that dwells within me.
>
> For I know that nothing good dwells within me, that is, in my flesh. I can will what is right, but I cannot do it.
>
> For I do not do the good I want, but the evil I do not want is what I do.[16]

One does not have to be Christian or even to be religious to recognize that human beings may be driven by "disordered desires," as Augustine called them. Unlike the Enlightenment thinkers who declared human beings naturally good, de Botton argues that the doctrine of original sin is useful even for atheists, because it encourages us to improve ourselves, understanding that the faults we note in ourselves are innately human, "inevitable features of the species." By thinking of ourselves as "fellow sinners," de Botton says, we can recognize that we are "beset by identical anxieties, temptations toward iniquity, cravings for love, and occasional aspirations to purity."[17]

More important, perhaps, the idea of original sin can help us understand, even if we do not share, some of the dark impulses we see in people throughout our own stories, and in our lives. Perhaps there are no monsters, only human beings. Some are good guys; some are bad; many are both, sometimes on the same day, just as we are. Rowan Williams argues that "even vile and murderous actions tend to come from somewhere, and if they are extreme in character we are not wrong to look for extreme situations. It does not mean that those who do them had no choice, are not answerable; far from it. But there is sentimentality too in ascribing what we don't understand to 'evil'; it lets us off the hook, it allows us to avoid the question of what, if anything, we can recognize in the destructive act of another."[18] That recognition of our own worst tendencies is a valuable feature of these stories. In "Your Own Worst Enemy," Bruce Springsteen, looking at post-9/11 American culture, sings that we may look in the mirror and realize that we have become the people we used to fear—may have become them, in fact, in response to the monsters we sought to survive. Nietzsche too famously warned that he or she who fights with monsters may become one in response.

In a world without limits, men and women can do what they have the will to do, can impose their wills to the limits of their power. While there are clear differences between Ramsay

Bolton and Rick Grimes, both are powerful men in a world where the dead walk and society is collapsing or has collapsed around them. Ramsay takes a sadistic pleasure in the horrible things he does; Rick takes no pleasure in the horrible things he does. Ramsay exults in violence and in chaos; Rick almost loses his mind in response to it. Ramsay rapes, tortures, and kills because it suits his desires as well as his call to power; Rick kills because he feels he has to in order to protect himself and those he serves. As Mario Loyola has written in the *National Review*, Rick's brutality sometimes stuns those who witness it, "but because he is guided by ethical reason as well as sometimes desperate passion, he preserves his humanity amid the barbarism to which man descends in the zombie apocalypse."[19]

To the dead, perhaps it makes little difference what motivations their killers have, or whether it is a matter of enjoyment or pain to them. But for us, thinking about the ethics of zombie tales, it matters a great deal. We tend to judge differently those who reluctantly do what they do not want to do in service of a larger ideal. Ramsay Bolton is ultimately only in service to himself; Rick is trying to preserve his community. But we must not pretend that there is no moral cost even to those who do bad things for what they believe to be a good reason. A former CIA operative involved with enhanced interrogation after 9/11 has said: "When you cross over that line of darkness, it's hard to come back. You lose your soul. You can do your best to justify it, but it's well outside the norm. You can't go to that dark a place without it changing you."[20]

When you go to the Dark Side, it can be hard to return. Actions have consequences. And so the person who returns may not be the same one who departed.

"WE DO WHAT WE NEED TO DO": BAD ACTS, GOOD INTENTIONS

> In this life now you kill or you die. Or you die and you kill.
> —THE GOVERNOR (DAVID MORRISSEY), *The Walking Dead*

As we've already discovered, the man and the boy in *The Road* have a running conversation about the ethics of the apocalypse. They agree that it's wrong to consume their fellow human beings at any time, but the boy struggles with some of his father's other guidance because in the course of their daily lives, they sometimes must make choices that seem to violate their code. When they take food or possessions they find on the road, the boy needs to be reassured that the people who own them are dead, that they are not simply stealing from others who are in need as they are. He even wants to hear that those owners would want them to take it. Yes, his father reassures him. They would. Just like we would want them to if the situation were reversed. Because we're the good guys, and so were they.[21] Still, the boy has a child's unbending moral code and sense of fairness. "If you break little promises you'll break big ones," the boy reminds his father. "That's what you said."[22] And on their journey, as they try simultaneously to find food and avoid becoming someone else's meal, promises get broken.

When the man shoots that stranger from the truck who has threatened them, the boy is covered with his blood, a visual representation of the guilt that splashes across them both. The man is not a killer, but as he tells the boy, he will do whatever he has to to keep him alive: "My job is to take care of you. I was appointed to do that by God. I will kill anyone who touches you."[23] This does not mean that the man has not also been affected by the killing; it simply means that he has made an ethical concession common to the Zombie Apocalypse. Just as Wichita in *Zombieland* says that she will do anything to keep her sister alive, many "good" characters in these zombie narratives do things they would never have done under less extreme circumstances. They compromise moral beliefs. They become more fearful, more calculating, more suspicious than they would wish, all in service of keeping themselves and those they love alive. Like the man, they have this mission, and within reason, they will do whatever it takes to survive. As Shane tells Rick in the "18 Miles Out" episode of season 2 of *The Walking Dead*, "You can't just be the good guy and expect to live." For many of the survivors of the Zombie Apocalypse the difficult choices arise out of that formulation: You can do the right thing, or what once was the right thing.

Or you can be dead.

Sometimes those choices seem almost obscene. Early in *The Walking Dead* story, Rick, who does not yet understand the change that has happened to his world while he lay in a coma, accuses his rescuer Morgan of murder: "You shot that man today."

"He was a walker," Morgan explains, and Rick begins to learn that one can and must kill these creatures that look human—so human, in fact, that Morgan finds himself unable to shoot his zombie wife until she has done great harm. Killing zombies themselves is psychologically difficult: their close resemblance to humans makes it seem as if survivors are transgressing another great taboo, despite the fact the zombies have no such compunctions about attacking them. This explains Morgan's hesitation and that of others in these stories. Consider Andrea (Laurie Holden) in season 1 of *The Walking*

Dead, cradling the dead body of her sister Amy (Emma Bell) and finally being forced to put a bullet in her brain when she reanimates. Think of Shaun in the Winchester, forced to help put his mum down as she changes. Remember Archie Andrews, Riverdale's all-American boy, weeping as he beats in his zombie father's skull with a baseball bat. Even killing nameless and anonymous zombies comes with a psychic toll; some of the zombie-killing professional soldiers who are interviewed in the book *World War Z* are shadows of their old selves, self-medicating or suicidal. Psychologist Colt J. Blunt theorizes that since the act of killing is the most traumatic known to us, no survivor in the world of the Zombie Apocalypse who has killed, whether zombies or other survivors, would escape psychic trauma.[24] It is a hard thing to kill, even to save your own life.

A harder choice has to do with killing the infected. Selena insists in *28 Days Later* that you have only ten or twenty seconds to put down those who contract the Rage virus or they will turn and kill you, that you have to do it no matter who has been infected. But these too are often emotionally difficult moments. Later in *28 Days Later*, no one seems to want to kill Frank, infected at the barrier, and it is sheer good fortune (in that respect, at least) that Major Hill's soldiers are present to put him down. In *Dawn of the Dead*, we have seen how Peter waits to kill Roger when he rises—and that painful action's significance is marked in the story by Francine's haunting question "It's really all over, isn't it?" Early in *The Walking Dead*, Rick and the group agree to leave the infected Jim behind rather than terminate his existence. It seems easier, less painful, than doing what needs to be done, what in later times they might do without thinking: preemptively killing him and assuring that he doesn't rise as a possible menace.

In season 2, when Dale is attacked by a walker and there is no hope he will survive, Rick finds he cannot shoot him. But Daryl can, and does, do what is necessary.

In *The Passage*, Agent Wolgast and Amy are discovered in their postapocalypse hideout by Bob, a man who has been infected with the virus, who pleads with Wolgast to kill him before he turns:

> "You're going to do this thing, aren't you?" Bob said. He was looking away, into the trees.
>
> "Yes," Wolgast said. "I'm sorry."
>
> "That's all right. Don't beat yourself up about it." He breathed heavily, licking his lips. He turned and touched his chest as Carl had done, all those months ago, to show Wolgast where to shoot. "Right through here, okay? You can shoot me through the head first, if you want, but make sure you put one in here."…
>
> "You can tell your daughter I drew on you," he added. "She shouldn't know about this. And burn the body when you're done."[25]

Even though Bob has asked him to do this thing, has a remarkably sane and forgiving attitude about it—and even though he begins to turn into one of the virals before Wolgast's very eyes—Wolgast is still haunted by this action, so akin to the murder we are commanded not to commit. He burns the body, and after discovering the snowmobile Bob rode into the mountains and his wallet with pictures of his family, the mourning Wolgast buries the wallet beneath a handmade cross. "It didn't seem like much, but it was all he could think to do."[26] These killings may be necessary, but though Wolgast and others can understand this rationally they are still profoundly affected by the actions they are forced to take.

Those who bear responsibility for others are also called to make compromises with their personal ethics in the new world. In the novel *World War Z*, a number of interviews record the hard choices that leaders made in order to preserve the largest number of their people. In his evacuation plan, South African strategist Paul Redeker said that the first casualty of the war against the zombies would have to be sentimentality; human emotion would lead to human extinction.[27] A German general, obeying similar tenets, orders his troops to pull out and leave civilians to be slaughtered and turned; in India, another military decision has refugees bombed by nerve gas in order to separate the infected from the clean, who will simply die and not revive. As one of the Germans who participated in the retreat puts it, "you have to make your own choices and live every agonizing day with the consequences of those choices."[28]

Likewise, while the boy in *The Road* and many of us believe there is such a thing as truth and its opposite is a lie, truth may be another casualty of the overwhelming menace. In *World War Z*, a Hollywood producer making propaganda films about the conflict admits to taking a selective approach to the facts in order to give his audiences hope. "Lies are neither bad nor good. Like a fire, they can either keep you warm or burn you to death."[29]

Summary executions are not simply the province of monsters in the world of the living dead; sometimes they are the result of agonizing decisions. In the "Judge, Jury, Executioner" episode of season 2 of *The Walking Dead*, Rick brings Randall in front of the group. Randall belongs to another large and well-armed group of survivors, and Rick declares him to be a threat. "You can't just decide on your own to take someone's life," Dale objects, and when the majority agree that Randall must die, Dale protests that they have lost their humanity. Only when Rick's son Carl expresses eagerness to witness the execution is it stopped. In season 5, however, Rick has become more pragmatic, more preemptive. He will kill without hesitation if it will save the others. So it is that in the episode "Strangers" he tells Father Gabriel that he knows the priest has a secret, and if what he is hiding hurts the others, he will not hesitate to kill him.

Later that season, Rick and Carol discuss Pete, one of the survivors in Alexandria, who is beating his wife. They agree that he should be executed. But when Rick goes to Deanna, the leader of the community, she forbids it. It is uncivilized, she responds; if worst came to worst, they would exile Pete. However, later in that episode—"Try"—Rick and Pete fight, and as the community gathers around them, Rick explains his stance on the efficacy of violence, how sometimes you have to do bad things in hopes of a good outcome. Unlike the citizens of Alexandria, his group knows that sometimes you have to make painful compromises to avoid even more painful casualties:

> We know what needs to be done and we do it. We're the ones who live. You, you just sit and plan and hesitate.... You wish things weren't what they are. Well, you want to live? You want this place to keep standing? Your way of doing things is done. Things don't get better because you—you want them to. Starting right now, we have to live in the real world....
>
> Your way is gonna destroy this place. It's gonna get people killed. It's already gotten people killed. I'm not gonna stand by and just let it happen. If you don't fight, you die.

Ethicist Scott Bader-Saye argues that in our post-9/11 situation we too are in a "real world" dominated by two binary choices, preemption or disengagement. Fear, he says, leads us to one of these two basic choices: either we "preemptively attack, seeking to destroy the source of our fear or to cause it to contract in the face of our threat. We are willing (some would say required) to strike first if it means we will become safer," or we voluntarily withdraw from engagements that may endanger us, praising ourselves for "wise self-limitation, although this looks a lot like cowardice." In either case, he says, we are hoping to neutralize our own fear.[30]

So sometimes our difficult choice is to choose preemption, to execute or attack in order, we think, to protect ourselves. And sometimes in a world filled with dangers, inaction becomes the logical—if difficult—ethical choice that allows one to go on living. The *Zombieland* rule "Don't be a hero" is geared to the latter way of thinking. Discretion may, in fact, sometimes be the better part of valor; certainly some characters discover times when they believe that it's better to do nothing than to expose themselves to danger. In *Night of the Living Dead*, Harry refuses to let Ben back inside after the pickup truck burns, believing, perhaps, that to open the door to Ben will further endanger him and his family (or perhaps he believes that having Ben in the house will offer further peril). In *28 Weeks Later*, Don (Robert Carlyle) flees, leaving his wife to die in a zombie attack; when she is later found alive, a nonsymptomatic carrier of the Rage virus, he rightly apologizes to her—and in one of that film's deep ironies, when she bestows a forgiving kiss, he is stricken by the same fate he had tried so hard to escape.

Manuel Gonzales's short story "Escape from the Mall" gives us Cowboy, the narrator, a not-so-heroic character who is thrust into the role of hero and not necessarily liking it. He and the others in their group have climbed up into the ceiling to try to escape the zombies who have trapped them in a closet. At one point he comes upon another of his group: "I see Francis the security guard ahead of me, struggling to pull himself back into the ceiling. Suddenly we seem to be surrounded by weak or weakened ceiling tiles. I think that I should help Francis, my security guard friend, but I have no desire to go down with that big ship. I slip past him. I feel bad for it, but that's what I do."[31]

In *The Road*, the boy and his father encounter others who, like themselves, are in difficult straits. "Can't we help him?" the boy often asks. His father's answer, typically, is that they can't. If they share their resources, they'll run out of food. It's also possible that a lone traveler is a decoy, a trap set for people like them. So they pass by a man struck by lightning, a starving dog, a little boy, and they travel on without stopping to help. At last, they encounter a starving old man, and the boy insists that this time they do what is right. How can you claim to be a good guy if you don't do good things? As Aristotle once put it, action is character. How can you claim to have virtues when you never demonstrate them?

In another difficult situation in *The Road*, the basement filled with humans being kept as cattle, the only safe choice for the father and son is to run for their lives, but that inaction still haunts the boy, who later lies with his head in his father's lap and asks:

> They're going to kill those people, aren't they?
> Yes.
> Why do they have to do that?
> I don't know.
> Are they going to eat them?
> I don't know.
> They're going to eat them, aren't they?

Yes.
And we couldn't help them because then they'd eat us too.
Yes.
And that's why we couldn't help them.
Yes.
Okay.[32]

Often, characters make these calculations out of fear: fear of scarcity, fear of violence, fear of consequences, fear of complexity. Columbus prefers to be on his own in *Zombieland* because he fears others, fears relationship, and fears that nothing good can come out of community, since he has never known anything good to emerge from it. In *The Road*, the man watches the road and keeps an eye out for other people so that he can escape whatever might be coming for him and the boy. The boy asks, "If you're on the lookout all the time does that mean you're scared all the time?" The man's answer offers some insight on this type of reasoning: "Well. I suppose you have to be scared enough to be on the lookout in the first place. To be cautious. Watchful, . . . Maybe you should always be on the lookout. If trouble comes when you least expect it then maybe the thing to do is always expect it."[33]

Maggie and Glenn in season 2 of *The Walking Dead* have a conversation that also spotlights the role fear plays in dark times, the dark place it can lead you, and the difference between mere survival and real living. Maggie tells Glenn, "I don't want to be afraid of being alive."

"Being afraid is what has kept us alive."

"No, it's how we keep breathing."

Fear is a biological response that helps make it possible to keep performing other biological responses. But it is not related to the higher possibilities, to the things I've explored earlier that make us truly human. And yet fear drives decision-making in the Zombie Apocalypse, and arguably, as Bader-Saye has suggested, fear defines our decision-making in real life, both as individuals and as people within larger groups. If so, then reckoning with fear is an essential part of discussing ethics, and there is much we can learn from the ways self-serving decisions are made in these stories, and much that philosophical and theological teachings about fear can illuminate in them.

The seventeenth-century British political philosopher Thomas Hobbes placed fear at the heart of his understanding of governments and of individual human behavior; for Hobbes, survival was the paramount human drive, and nothing could be worse than a world unraveled by war, the threat of violence, or, one supposes, an overrunning horde of the walking dead. In such a world, Hobbes wrote in his hugely influential work *Leviathan*, there can be "No Arts; No Letters; no Society; and which is worst of all, continuall feare, and danger of violent death; And the life of man, solitary, poore, nasty, brutish, and short."[34] For those in *The Road*, *The Walking Dead*, *28 Days Later*, and many other stories of the Zombie Apocalypse, this is an accurate accounting of the life they can expect: solitary, poor, nasty, brutish, and short. Who would not be afraid in such a world? Continual fear, Hobbes concludes, is worse than all other calamities, and fear drives people to compromises and actions they might not otherwise take.

Thus in the Zombie Apocalypse, we see the inaction of good people, and the sometimes contradictory actions of people who maintain that they know better. The man, who is teaching his son to carry the fire, stands aside when he might save others, and he conserves resources when he might share them. At last, in a heartbreaking scene, he takes back at gunpoint everything stolen from them by a starving man.

All of this is caused by the fear that he will not be able to protect his son. In a final exchange, the two men debate survival ethics:

> Don't do this, man.
> You didn't mind doing it to us.
> I'm begging you.
> Papa, the boy said.
> Come on. Listen to the kid.
> You tried to kill us.
> I'm starving, man. You'd have done the same.
> You took everything.
> Come on, man. I'll die.
> I'm going to leave you the way you left us.[35]

And so the man leaves the thief shivering naked in the road. As a result of this action, the boy survives for a little longer. But what, we wonder, is the soul cost of this fear?

Many modern philosophers, although differing from each other in religious beliefs, political affiliations, and attitudes on war, follow Hobbes in placing fear at the heart of human decision-making. The twentieth-century British philosopher and liberal politician Bertrand Russell, an atheist, wrote in a tract entitled "War: The Offspring of Fear" that otherwise reasonable people—and nations—might do all sorts of things when they are terrified, since "the one motive that makes the populations acquiesce is fear."[36] In this pacifist criticism of his nation's involvement in World War I, he argued that the "universal reign of fear" was to blame for the binding military alliances that had pulled the Western nations into senseless conflict, that these "immense forces of heroism and devotion [were] destroying each other through a tragedy of blindness and fear," and that if civilization were to survive, a cure must be found for the universal fear that caused such "mutual butchery."[37]

Although he came at life from a very different perspective, the twentieth-century Catholic monk and activist Thomas Merton agreed with Russell's conclusions. "At the root of all war," Merton said, "is fear: not so much the fear men have of one another as the fear they have of everything."[38] Perhaps, he says, your enemy "is afraid of you because he feels that you are afraid of him."[39] Human beings have the tendency to perceive those who think, act, and believe differently as a threat, and those on both sides are united in their fear of each other—although, of course, much more strongly divided by that fear. The end result is violence.

In our own time, conservative Christian ethicist Jean Bethke Elshtain has written that people always live with fear, although, like Russell, she hopes that we will not act solely out of it. "One must not give oneself over to [fear]," she writes. "When one capitulates to this fear, one gets horrible wars of destruction."[40] Although Elshtain, unlike Russell and Merton, concludes that sometimes evil can only be confronted with force, she falls back on the power of reason even in the grip of fear. Wendy Murray Zoba writes that "in these times, when the fear of unregulated violence hovers in people's consciousness, Elshtain is trying to think through risks and options in the light of moral conscience."[41]

Moral conscience is important, because few good outcomes stem from fear, and many bad ones. Typically it engages our most destructive tendencies and disengages our creative faculties. "*I must not fear,*" chants a character in Frank Herbert's classic novel *Dune*. "*Fear is the mind-killer*"— good spiritual advice from the most popular science fiction novel of all time.[42] It is also good political and psychological advice; frightened people make poor citizens and poor human beings. When we are afraid, threats seem magnified, our ability to deal with them creatively seems reduced, and our range of options seems limited. Thus philosophers, artists, theologians, and wise politicians have always warned of the danger of letting fear go unchecked. Franklin D. Roosevelt did not say "We ought to fear everything." He said, "The only thing we have to fear is fear itself."

Fear is a force in our lives—in our personal lives, in our social and political lives. We rarely talk about it, for to acknowledge it is to make our fears tangible. Yet when we pretend that those fears are not driving us—fail to recognize that we as individuals and as a nation have made the avoidance of fear our highest value—we do things we should not, and do not even know why we are doing them. Fear must be named if it is to be faced and solved. As Rowan Williams says, "to acknowledge the reality of fear is not to collude with it. But not to recognize how pervasive it is risks making it worse."[43]

So why, given the debilitating effects of fear, have leaders in our zombie stories and real-life politicians done their level best to make sure their constituents remained afraid? Perhaps exactly because when we are terrified, threats seem magnified and our range of options seems limited. When we are afraid, we may be moved, as Bader-Saye observes, to preemptively attack, to do unto others before they can do unto us.[44] Leaders can attempt to take advantage of these fears by drumming up support for conflicts. The nineteenth-century British statesman William Gladstone labeled the call to go to war against China "a false and illegitimate appeal. It is an appeal to fear, which is seldom a rightful and noble sentiment."[45] Perhaps not, but Americans after 9/11 likewise seemed willing to favor martial claims in the hope that they might achieve—or regain—a sense of safety. If we did to them first, perhaps we could prevent another attack on New York, another attack on Washington, or other much-feared but vaguely realized kinds of attack on us and our families.

In *World War Z*, the Zombie Apocalypse is known as "The Great Panic," and well it might be. When the world changes forever, fear, terror, and panic are obvious responses. The same holds true for 9/11. Since then, neither American political party has seemed able to articulate a vision that is not oriented toward terror and the nation's response to it. Back in 2005, political scientist Corey Robin told *New York* magazine: "Fear is the dominant, perhaps the only language of public life today. But [President George W.] Bush has help from the Democrats— they can't imagine a different way of justifying their power. The first thing [presidential candidate John] Kerry does at the [Democratic] convention is salute and say, 'I'm reporting for duty.' That's a reference to the fear that looks to the nation's enemies and the protection he'll provide."[46]

Our fear has made us willing to embrace a wide variety of options we once would have shunned; fear operates in the same way in the ravaged world of the Zombie Apocalypse. Fear makes some survivors in *The Walking Dead* embrace the Governor as their leader, thinking that though his methods may be frightening the threats facing Woodbury are more frightening still. The Governor may be one of the most reviled characters in contemporary culture, but it's not because he fails in his goal of creating a stable and relatively safe society in the midst of the zombie outbreak. Even Andrea, who has been part of Rick's group since before his arrival outside Atlanta, is drawn to the Governor and chooses to stay in Woodbury, at least until she discovers what the Governor is doing to her friends.

The example of the Governor reminds us that if we do not grapple with our fears as well as with those who might actually attack us, we are faced with a future dedicated to our new gods of safety and security, with fealty owed to whoever can deliver them. Whatever we make our highest goods will define our lives, and if safety and security replace compassion and hospitality and justice as our highest goods, then we will continue to make decisions privileging safety and security over those virtues. "In a culture of fear," Bader-Saye writes, "the short answer to 'What is going on?' is 'We are at risk' or 'We are in danger.'" If this is what we believe, then our lives will be oriented primarily toward the spiritually dubious value of self-preservation.[47] When Rick announces to the gathered people of Alexandria that the world has changed and the methods of staying safe in it have changed, he is exalting self-preservation, security, above all things. And it is a short step from saying "My security is paramount" to "I'll do some heinous things to preserve myself and the people I love."

When after the 9/11 attacks President George W. Bush said that the United States—like Rick, like the man—would use any means necessary to protect its citizens, and his ally Tony Blair stood by him to say Britain would support the United States, they committed two of the world's great democracies to a course of action that violated their core values. In the process, both nations lost a great store of their moral standing, while acting in the name of defending freedom and fighting evil. Both Bush and Blair identified themselves as Christians whose worldviews were shaped by their faith. John Gray has noted that in the theological reflections of both leaders on their conduct of the war, their good intentions justified these bad actions, trumping concerns about any secrecy or even deceit that might be required.[48]

It could be said that these leaders and their administrations were acting as those whom the theologian Reinhold Niebuhr, speaking of Cold Warriors during the long fight against Communism, called "realists": they are "inclined to argue that a good cause will hallow any weapon," he said, and are so convinced of the evil of the foe "that we are justified in using any weapon against them. Thereby they closely approach the communist ruthlessness."[49] When we go over to the Dark Side, Niebuhr suggests (and experience confirms), it is possible—indeed, likely—that we will become more, not less, like the implacable foes we oppose.

At a top-level international intelligence gathering in 2002, CIA director George Tenet said that the 9/11 attacks had altered old codes, thinking, and alliances. "As for the CIA," he said, "There's nothing we won't do, nothing we won't try, and no country we won't deal with to achieve our goals—to stop the enemy." He then named a number of nations formerly considered authoritarian or terrorist states with whom the United States would now be willing to ally itself.[50] In the face of this new danger the nation would do anything and work with anyone, no matter how ethically challenged we might consider them.

But, whether in real life or in its stand-in the Zombie Apocalypse, are these compromises worth making to achieve the noble end of survival? In the 2005 film *Good Night, and Good Luck*, Edward R. Murrow (David Strathairn), in the closing of a broadcast attacking Senator Joe McCarthy's anti-communist witch hunt, puts it thus: "We proclaim ourselves as indeed we are, the defenders of freedom wherever it still exists in the world. But we cannot defend freedom abroad by deserting it at home." The Judeo-Christian tradition has wrestled with this question of how we defend ourselves against an external menace and offers possible wisdom—as well as pit-falls that might snare us. As we seek an ethical response to the traumatic events of the past decade and to the characters in our stories, we might examine the spectrum of beliefs emerging from scripture and tradition.

Elsewhere in his book *The Irony of American History*, Niebuhr described two extremes of belief, which we might identify as Christian pacifism and holy war: "Our idealists are divided between those who would renounce the responsibilities of power for the sake of preserving the purity of our soul and those who are ready to cover every ambiguity of good and evil in our actions by the frantic insistence that any measure taken in a good cause must be unequivocally virtuous."[51] In other words, like Deanna (Tovah Feldshuh) in her initial reaction to Rick and his group as the leader of Alexandria's survivors, some would say that any compromise is one too many, while Rick defends the opposite view: "There's nothing we won't do, nothing we won't try," if it will keep us alive. A third option also emerges, however, when, like Niebuhr, we acknowledge that regrettably, power must be exercised in some conditions. We might call this the just war tradition, while Niebuhr (and President Barack Obama) called it "Christian realism."

These three divisions constitute the primary Christian understandings of power, conflict, and the use of violence. At his best, Rick seeks to balance the necessity of violence to protect himself and the survivors he leads with an ethical core he carries as one trained to protect, serve, and uphold the law. This is realism, avoiding the extremes. But the extremes are usually easier to adhere to, and certainly easier to depict.

As someone who has taught fiction- and screen-writing for over two decades, I can anticipate the scene in which two characters debate, like Rick and Deanna, the ethical choices behind execution, preemptive attacks, enhanced interrogation, and other morally dubious practices that may or may not lead to greater safety.

"If we take up the enemy's methods," one character would say, "then how are we better than the enemy?" (Or like Dale, earlier in the show, we might ask, "If we do this, how can we not lose our humanity?")

The response from the other, naturally, sounds like this: "Don't be naïve. I didn't make this world. I'm just trying to live in it. And the only way to live in it is to make these hard choices, to strike them before they strike you." (Like Shane, we might ask, Do you think you can be an old-fashioned hero and survive in these bad lands?)

Violence is a useful dramatic tool. As a writer and teacher of narrative, I can affirm that it is almost always more interesting for characters to engage in violent conflict than for them to debate the ethics of engaging in violent conflict. But the stories of the Zombie Apocalypse also offer us substantial numbers of people making ethical choices in spite of fear, in spite of their strong drive for self-preservation. Sometimes, in the face of overwhelming danger, human beings still manage to do the right thing, and in the final section of this chapter I'll consider some of those ethical choices that mark us as truly human—and consider whether or not violence as a tool helps or ultimately hinders us as we seek not just to go on breathing, but to live.

"LIGHT UP THE DARKNESS": DOING THE RIGHT THING

In that heartbreaking scene near the end of *The Road* where the father, whom we have grown to admire for his strength and his care for his son, takes back all the supplies another man has stolen from him, readers and viewers often feel a visceral reaction and a powerful sense of conflict: on the one hand we understand the fear that drives him, the love that impels him to do whatever he must to protect his son. We too want the boy to survive, or else what has our own suffering in this narrative been for? On the other hand a part of us looks at that man, who has tried to teach his son the right way to survive in a world full of violence and scarcity, and we think to ourselves: *You are better than this.*

In fact, the one bright spot is that the boy is able to prevail on his father not to kill the thief. He begs him not to, and his father listens. (He has also begged his father not to leave the thief nude and shivering in the road, which his father has ignored.) Afterward, the boy cannot stop crying, even after they have gone on up the road. "Just help him, Papa, just help him," he pleads.

> The man looked back up the road.
> He was just hungry, Papa. He's going to die.
> He's going to die anyway.
> He's so scared, Papa.
> The man squatted and looked at him. I'm scared, he said.
> Do you understand? I'm scared.

We can imagine a version of that made-up scene where goodness and pragmatism wrestle: *If we don't help him, he'll die. We have to do what's right.*

If we do help him, we'll die. We don't live in a world where Goodness can survive.

The man tells the boy that the boy is not the one who has to worry about everything. The response is surprising: "Yes I am, he said. I am the one."[52]

When the man speaks of "everything," he means the world of the physical: the threat of starvation, hypothermia, rape, murder. He has spent the entire novel worrying about, planning against, dreading the physical challenges of keeping them both alive and breathing. But when the boy speaks of "everything," he seems to mean something else, something higher, something more spiritual than physical. Certainly it is the boy who is the voice of compassion throughout the book, worrying not only about himself and his father but also about all those they encounter along the way: the emaciated dog, the little boy, the lightning-struck man, the old vagabond, even the thief who would have left them for dead. It is the boy who continually asks his father about bad guys and good guys, who constantly seeks reassurance that they are good guys.

As impractical as it might be, the boy is worried—even in this fallen world, where peril lies around every corner—about doing the right thing.

I have taught Spike Lee's 1989 film *Do the Right Thing* on many occasions, both in film classes at Baylor University and in parish settings. Whenever I teach this profoundly dualist work, which presents on the one hand the vision of Dr. Martin Luther King, Jr., and the way of nonviolence and on the other the vision of Malcolm X, famous for saying he would advance the black cause by any means necessary, ethical questions rise to the fore. In the film, some characters employ violence or threat; some preach peace and love; none ends up completely happy at story's end. Da Mayor (Ossie Davis) early on tells Spike Lee's Mookie to "always do the right thing." But what, in a divided, conflicted, and dangerous world, *is* the right thing?

Do the Right Thing has no easy answers to that question, any more than we find easy answers in the stories of the Zombie

Apocalypse, or in our own lives, for that matter. We are conditioned to want to survive in the face of heavy odds, and culturally we are conditioned to look out for ourselves; radical individualism makes it difficult to want to care for others, particularly those not attached to us by economic or familial ties. Yet the Zombie Apocalypse also contains stories of people setting aside their fear, reaching out to others, and doing the right thing, whatever it might cost them. Realistic it may not be, for as Reinhold Niebuhr argued, a nation (or perhaps, in our context, a community's leader) can't choose peace and sacrificial compassion, because it may lead to that nation's destruction. "We take, and must continue to take, morally hazardous actions to preserve our civilization. We must exercise our power," he argued in response to the fear and threats of the Cold War.[53] In the context of the Zombie Apocalypse, it's difficult to see how one responds to Major Hill or Negan or the zombie hordes with compassion and forbearance; yet we also return to the conversation between Glenn and Maggie about the difference between existing and truly living, the boy's concern about good guys and bad guys.

Is that life of fear, constriction, and preemptive violence truly worth living—in the world of the Zombie Apocalypse or in our own world—even if it preserves our lives?

We have seen how in a world without rules, some people choose the unforgivable: control, torture, and execution. Others make morally hazardous choices to attack, kill, or withhold actions or resources when to offer them might endanger themselves or their tribe. In this final section on ethics, we will seek some answers to what it means to do the right thing, what it might mean to carry the light in a world full of darkness. Scott Bader-Saye offers us a counterweight to Harry Potter's Unforgivable Curses, suggesting three noble actions we should offer even though they may be counter-intuitive in a culture of fear: hospitality, peacemaking, and generosity.[54]

Hospitality is about our response to the strange—or to the stranger. Will we react with fear, hostility, even violence? Or will we greet each stranger as a fellow human being with the potential to carry the light? "Namaste," the traditional Hindu greeting, means something like "The divine spirit in me acknowledges the divine spirit within you." Hospitality is about welcome, about setting aside fear and partisanship, about recognizing our common humanity. In the movie *World War Z,* Gerry is taken in by a family, rescued despite his potential to be dangerous or a carrier of the virus. When the parents of young Tomas (Fabrizio Zacharee Guido) are bitten and turn, Gerry takes Tomas with him and cares for him as his own. So too, in *28 Days Later*, Selena rescues Jim, and Frank and Hannah later welcome the two of them although they do not know each other and these rescues may offer more danger than benefit.

In *The Walking Dead*, while the scope of Hershel's hospitality is limited to the time it takes Carl to get better, he does offer a group of strangers the chance to stay on his farm. Later in the story, Michonne shows up brandishing a sword and leading two zombies in chains, an entrance that would certainly make me think twice about future relationship, but Rick offers the safety of the prison to her. Deanna and the people of Alexandria welcome Rick and his group behind their walls and, in the most homely yet tangible way, welcome them with human touches like haircuts. In all these cases and more, people set aside their justifiable fear and take the chance on relationship by offering hospitality.

In the world of *Game of Thrones*, hospitality is considered a cardinal virtue, and the violations of that code lead to some of the moments of greatest horror in the story, reminding us that hospitality should be an essential ethical responsibility. Strangers are to be offered bread and salt, and once that has been consumed, they are supposed to be safe among their hosts and hostesses. The Red Wedding, where Walder Frey (David Bradley) murders a number of his guests at dinner, is deservedly seen as one of the most villainous events in the Song of Ice and Fire saga. To extend hospitality and then violate it is against all the laws of human decency. As in the case of the cannibals of Terminus in *The Walking Dead*, who feast on those who come to them for help, or the soldiers at the Barrier in *28 Days Later* who betray those who arrive seeking sanctuary, it is a rank sin against humanity to take advantage of your guests.

Once he becomes Lord Commander of the Night's Watch, Jon Snow alarms his men in season 5 by offering hospitality to their traditional enemies, the Wildlings from north of the Wall. "The long night is coming," he tells them, "and the dead come with it." In extending hospitality to these tribes, or in seeking to rescue those Wildlings beset by undead wights at Hardhome, he is remembering that against the threat of the living dead, the living must stick together. They have much more in common with each other than with their common foe. As Sam explains to Ollie, "I've seen the army of the dead. I've seen the White Walkers. And they're coming for us, for all the living.... And when it's time, we'll need every last man we can find."

Afterlife with Archie offers a delicious scene in which the heroic Archie has banded the survivors together and brought them to Lodge Manor, Veronica's house, the mansion built and presided over by her father (and Archie's long-time nemesis), Hiram Lodge. As Veronica tells her father about the horrifying events of the evening—Jughead's attack on Ethel at the dance, the transformation of many of their friends and acquaintances to zombies, their escape, she encourages him to come with her into the main hall, "and please...don't lose your temper."[55]

There Mr. Lodge finds Archie, Betty, Moose, and Midge, and other teens who have escaped the slaughter and are seeking refuge at Lodge Manor. Although Veronica worried about her father's reaction, to his credit, there doesn't seem to be a moment's hesitation. He offers them haven, and more, extending his paternal care to them as though they were his own children. Shortly after the teens arrive, Mr. Lodge asks his butler, Smithers, for a status report, concluding with the most important question: "Are all the children safe? And accounted for?"[56] Later, after the zombie virus has been brought within the walls and two of the teens have been turned, the always-chilly Mr. Lodge betrays unsuspected humanity, saying, "Two more of them lost, Smithers, on my watch. What will I tell their mothers and fathers...?"[57]

It would have been easier perhaps to turn away Veronica's friends, to have taken care of himself and his household, or he might have taken them in grudgingly, only to appease his daughter. But Mr. Lodge, like many characters in the Zombie Apocalypse, goes well beyond doing nothing, or doing the minimum. He recognizes a human responsibility to be compassionate, one that has been enshrined in our wisdom traditions as well as in our stories. Compassion is a central virtue in Buddhism, to be extended to all, and it helps guide us to ethical decisions. "So far as ethics is concerned," the Dalai Lama has written, "where love of one's neighbor, affection, kindness, and compassion live, we find that ethical conduct is automatic. Ethically wholesome actions arise naturally in the context of compassion."[58]

In the desert traditions from which both Muslims and Jews draw meaning, hospitality to the stranger was automatic. When a stranger stood outside one's home—or one's tent—he or she was to be welcomed in, fed, their feet washed. A failure of hospitality was to be memorialized and lamented; many scholars believe that the destruction of Sodom and Gomorrah in the Book of Genesis has much less to do with homosexuality than with the epic failure of hospitality when citizens demand that Lot send the strangers he has welcomed out to them to be raped.

The Hebrew Bible contains many verses on how the poor, the widow, the orphan, and the stranger are to be treated, and the prophets' many calls to justice revolve around failures to extend hospitality and generosity to those who are most in need. It may seem strange that tribal people would codify the need to welcome the alien, yet this is a moral imperative that extends into the Christian tradition. In the Benedictine Rule, for example, monks and sisters are urged to welcome every stranger as though he or she is Christ himself.[59] Although the Benedictine Rule was codified during the Middle Ages, a time full of terror and chaos, for these faithful people the response to any human being who showed up at their gates was to be radical welcome.

Does hospitality produce a force field guarding those who extend it from violence or otherwise being taken advantage of? Of course not, any more than any of the forms of compassion I'm discussing here do; for the truly monstrous, for Negan, for the Governor, for those cannibals overseeing the slaughterhouse in the cellar of their house, for Walder Frey, for all of those who are sidestepping normal human behaviors, compassion and generosity will be taken as weakness. But for those operating in the second sphere I've considered—the man in *The Road*, Rick, or any of those who would like to do the right thing but are afraid that it may have terrible consequences—compassion extended may mean compassion returned. The same, we trust, might be said for peacemaking and generosity as well, the other cardinal virtues to be cultivated in a time of fear and danger.

Rick's contempt for the lack of martial skills of the people of Alexandria seems to be shared by the other people from his group, and perhaps by the audience of *The Walking Dead*. It is Carol who tells Rick, in the season 5 episode "Spend," that Pete needs to be dealt with preemptively before he hurts anyone again: "You're gonna have to kill him." In "Try," Glenn tells the inept Alexandria scouts, who have lost some of their own outside their walls, that they are a danger to themselves and others: "Those four people you lost on that run, that's on you. People like you are supposed to be dead, but these walls went up just in time, so you're not. You don't go outside these walls anymore. Not by yourself, not with anyone else."

It is their skill with violence that makes Rick and his group useful to Deanna. When Father Gabriel (Seth Gilliam) tells Deanna that Rick and the others did unspeakable things out there, she replies, "They survived. That's what makes them assets." But violence is a limited skill set. There's truth to the old saying that when the only tool in your kit is a hammer, every problem looks like a nail. Violence has limitations as well as uses, and ultimately violence becomes an echo chamber that will burst your eardrums.

Peacemaking seems the least possible of the cardinal virtues. Can you discuss peace terms with a zombie? Can you peacefully defuse tensions with a gang who want your food, or your wife, or your shelter? No, of course not, and part of Deanna's realization is that although she is a person of peace, it may be necessary to have someone around who can counter violence with violence. But the task of peacemaking, naïve as it sometimes seems (did you make peace with Hitler, Neville Chamberlain?), is likewise a virtue, for it enjoins us to treat other humans as creatures worthy of our engagement, and to mark them as people potentially bearing the light whom we must not kill if we do not need to. Christian ethicist Stanley Hauerwas, once named by *Time* as America's preeminent theologian, places peacemaking at the center of his work. In *The Peaceable Kingdom*, he argues that "peaceableness as the hallmark of Christian life helps illumine other issues, such as the nature of moral argument, the meaning and status of freedom, as well as how religious convictions can be claimed to be true or false."[60] Peacemaking is an ethical practice that can shape other ethical practices, if we only attempt it.

In the second episode of *The Walking Dead*, Rick makes a decision with far-reaching consequences. Although he judges Merle to be violent, bigoted, and a danger to the group, he chooses not to kill him. Instead, he "imprisons" him, securing him to a pipe on the roof of a downtown building while the others carry out their mission in Atlanta. It would have been easier to kill him, and Merle, overcoming great hardships, not only escapes but pops up in their lives again to cause problems. But this early in the story, Rick still believes that you should only do violence when you absolutely have to, and Merle is allowed to live as a result.

In the season 1 episode "Tell It to the Frogs," Merle's brother Daryl might have killed Rick if he had learned that they had executed his brother. When Daryl hears that his brother has been left on a rooftop, he attacks Rick with a knife. But Rick and Shane disarm Daryl, and although again Rick might be justified in killing (Daryl has tried to take his life, and he might try again), he tells Daryl instead that he wants to talk this through. They go back to try to rescue Merle, although Shane asks Rick why he'd risk his life for a guy who "wouldn't give you a glass of water if you were dyin' of thirst."

Because, Rick says, "I can't let a man die of thirst.... We left him like an animal caught in a trap. That's no way for anything to die, let alone a human being."

While there is life, there is always possibility. If Rick had killed Daryl, he would have been cut down at the lowest point of his moral development. The Daryl who saves Rick and the others with his skill and his hunting, the Daryl who feeds Rick's infant daughter, the Daryl whom Rick calls "my brother," would never have existed. Here is a case where peacemaking clearly shows it has the potential to change the world for the better.

From a narrative point of view we have to acknowledge that peacemaking may not be an effective story element, particularly with thousands of zombies, wights, walkers, or virals stalking around just outside our walls. To refuse to kill them would subject audiences, readers, or gamers to hours of unnecessary tedium. But as an exercise connected to other human beings, both in the Zombie Apocalypse and in our own, peacemaking does, as Hauerwas notes, pose a number of questions worthy of our consideration.

First, precisely how much agency do we have in responding to the threats we perceive? Will our violence end those threats? If so, is that end temporary or permanent? It has become a trope in *The Walking Dead* that Rick and his group encounter one or a few members of a larger group, violence breaks out, and it results in an even larger conflict, often with lethal results for characters we love. But in Christian understanding—and in the world of the Zombie Apocalypse—love is the ultimate faithful response to a world full of pain, fear, and conflict. Holy war can perhaps strike down some of the foes of a country or of a belief; a just war can perhaps preserve a nation or community for a season. But ultimately, neither can destroy the abiding hatred that causes war. Think of Adolf Hitler, a defeated German soldier who arose out of the embers of World War I more filled with hate than ever. Think of today's neo-Nazis, still following the racist and supremacist creeds of Hitler seventy years after *his* death. Violence only feeds the cycle of violence, fear, and hatred. As Martin Luther King, Jr., preached, "darkness cannot drive out darkness; only light can do that. Hate cannot drive out hate; only love can do that. Hate multiplies hate, violence multiplies violence."[61] Likewise the Dalai Lama writes: "violence can achieve certain short-term objectives, but it cannot obtain long-lasting ends."[62] Violence may be a tactical weapon against evil, but it is never a strategic one.

Certainly the Christian tradition encompasses the realism of Niebuhr, as well as the just war theory of Augustine and Aquinas. One can choose to counter deadly force with force and not regard it as evil or unethical. One might in fact argue, as Elshtain does, that we have a responsibility to act, that protecting the weak and the helpless is in its own way an ethical or even good action. But ultimately, ethicists from many traditions and from no tradition suggest that peace is a worthy goal.

We can see this in narrative terms in the way many zombie films end. If they don't conclude with the probable or actual death and destruction of the protagonists for whom we have rooted, they tend to end in moments of peace and relative tranquility. The battle is over. A small community has formed. Life goes on, and maybe now it can go on in a way that is better than it was before. So it is that, at the end of *28 Days Later*, we find Jim and Selena in a small cottage, where they are discovered by a NATO airplane and presumably rescued. At the end of *Zombieland*, the battle for the amusement park has ended, Tallahassee has his Twinkie, Columbus has his new family, and all is well.

What we all want—in story as in life—is an end to conflict, an end to fear, and hope that we can live together. Peacemaking may actually require more courage than making war, for it means giving up the illusion that our actions will be decisive in the grand scheme of things. Declining to make war does not mean simple inaction; peacemaking is a process, not an abdication of responsibility. The Christian pacifist John Howard Yoder argues that doing nothing was never an option for Jesus; we have only to look at the world in which he walked and spoke and healed and died to know that what Jesus did, whatever he chose, would have a social and political dimension. So if doing nothing was not an option, the two options remaining for him were seizing cultural power or exerting countercultural nonviolence: "The one temptation the man Jesus faced—and faced again and again and again—as a constitutive element of his public ministry, was the temptation to exercise social responsibility, in the interest of justified revolution, through the use of available violent methods."[63] He chose instead the way of nonviolence, but again, he had to choose, and to exert himself as actively in peace as he might have in war.

Peacemaking is not for the lazy, the weak, or the naïve; it requires the best of us, and all we have to offer. It tests us to our limits. In speaking about the cardinal virtues I've explored in this chapter, Bader-Saye notes how "courage is the capacity to do what is right and good in the face of fear. We become courageous when we learn to live for something that is more important than our own safety."[64] Making peace will require more courage than making war, because it will mean setting aside our natural impulses toward safety and security in the hope of something transformative.

The last of Bader-Saye's three ethical calls is to generosity—a reshaping of our priorities away from ourselves, our perceived needs and perceived scarcity, and toward a generous concern for others. The most recent story line of *Marvel Zombies* (as of this writing the 2015 story *Battleworld*) follows monster hunter Elsa Bloodstone, daughter of the legendary Ulysses Bloodstone, who taught her to make no peace with evil, and to root it out wherever she found it. In words that echo in her mind and in her life, he taught her it was "better to destroy what's good than to let the darkness devour it."[65] Although this story line features its share of familiar Marvel characters as flesh-eating zombies, the main characters of the Battleworld installment are human heroes fighting off hordes of the undead drawn together from across the Marvel multiverse. Elsa is one of many defending the Shield, a wall holding back the Zombie Apocalypse, when she is taken from her post by a superpowered zombie and flung far south of the wall into the Deadlands. There she encounters a single human child, whom she immediately christens "Shut Up" in honor of the words she most often directs toward the girl, before ordering her on a merciless march—and commanding her to stop crying.

Elsa Bloodstone's upbringing was horrific, and she is in the midst of a multidimensional onslaught of supercharged zombies. But in her interactions with the girl, Elsa begins to change. At first she speaks in terms of scarcity—there are only so many shells in the gun, so many emergency bags of tea, so many actions that can be taken, "and zombies. Lots and lots of zombies"—but then she begins to exhibit generosity.[66] Although taught by her father not to make the feeble her burden, she takes the girl in hand and protects her. Her father raised her from childhood to be self-sufficient and deadly, to feel no emotions and pay attention to nothing but her duty, but when she catches herself following his patterns she stops herself from treating the child in the same way. She curses the memory of her father and says, "Children should be children."[67] Responding to this seemingly useless stranger, Elsa Bloodstone defeats her tendencies toward brusqueness and distance, toward the use of violence as an all-purpose tool, and she begins to cultivate the qualities of empathy, compassion, and care.

Like the man in *The Road*, whom she grows to resemble (and perhaps is intended to resemble), Elsa accepts that her role is to protect this child entrusted to her although it goes against all her learned instincts. The child proves to be an ethical goad to her, causing her to take compassionate actions that seem counterproductive or even dangerous. At one point, although it will almost certainly mean their deaths, Elsa agrees with the child that they should destroy this reality's incarnation of Deadpool, an unfortunate wretch who because of his radical ability to heal has been suspended by zombies to serve as a sort of eternal buffet, eaten every night, restored by the next. Later, although she knows her duty lies back at the Shield and this child seems to have no utility against the zombie tide, she gives up her transport to try to send the girl to safety. She demonstrates generosity of resources, time, and action, and her growing unselfishness shines out for us so power-fully because all of these things are against her deeply learned behaviors—as they would be for many of us.

In the Christian tradition this willingness to show hospi-tality, to make peace where before there has been animosity, and to live with generosity is perhaps best exemplified in Jesus's parable of the Good Samaritan. In this story that would not be out of place in one of our zombie narratives, a Jewish man is assaulted by robbers and left for dead beside the road. Two holy men see him there and pass by on the other side of the road, afraid to stop, perhaps because they fear that they too might become victims, or that the fallen man is a decoy work-ing for robbers. It is, instead, a Samaritan, a member of a race long hated by the Jews, who stops to render aid. Without regard for his own safety, comfort, or convenience, he binds the man's wounds, lifts him onto his own donkey, and takes him to an inn, where he asks the innkeeper to take care of him. Anything he needs, the Samaritan says, give him, and I will repay you when I return.

On the night before he was assassinated, Martin Luther King, Jr., retold this story to a group of striking sanitation workers in Memphis, and it led him to talk about our fear and our selfishness. What we do when we are afraid, Dr. King said, is to ask the question "What will happen to me if I stop to help?" The truly ethical question, however, is this: "What will happen to them if I do not help?" The Samaritan, he said, represents a dangerous unselfishness, the willingness to extend himself for the benefit of another of God's children.[68] The soul in him was touched by the soul of his fallen brother, and their shared humanity could not be denied.

It is particularly hard to offer generosity in times of fear, for we are afflicted by our belief in scarcity. There is not enough—not enough food, not enough water, not enough space, not enough bullets, not enough tea—to go around, we think, whether we are characters beset by gangs and zombies or people facing a world filled with refugees, terrorists, the poor, the sick, and the suffering. This final goal for ethical behavior is also the third virtue we see represented by the boy in *The Road*. Not only does he seek to welcome those whom he and his father encounter on the road (perhaps a part of his drive to understand good guys and bad guys—if it's possible these are good guys, they may be carrying the fire as well, and so we should help them); he seeks to defuse tensions and keep his father from committing violence. He is constantly asking if something might be done for those they encounter. "Isn't there anything we can do to help them?" is his common question, leading to his father's reply "No. We don't have enough."

In his father's final hours—or perhaps in the father's dying delirium, for the narrative is unclear—they have a final conversation about the little boy they left behind on the road. The father was concerned, like the purportedly good men in the story of the Good Samaritan, that the boy was a trap, bait for an attack. The boy, of course, saw someone like himself, another human being in need.

Do you remember that little boy, Papa?
Yes. I remember him.
Do you think he's all right that little boy?
Oh yes. I think he's all right.
Do you think he was lost?
No. I don't think he was lost.
I'm scared that he was lost.
I think he's all right.

But who will find him if he's lost? Who will find the little
    boy?
Goodness will find the little boy. It always has. It will again.[69]

It does not seem likely; here he is, the man, the most ethical
creature we have encountered on *The Road*, yet a man capable of chilling violence and seeming amorality in service of
himself and his son, evoking the thin possibility of goodness
in a world of brutality and sure death. When the boy awakes
next to his father, the body is cold. The boy remains, weeping
next to his father, calling his name. After three days, he walks
out to the road, and the miraculous happens: there he encounters a man, scarred and armed, who nonetheless speaks
gently to him. He offers to take the boy with him, and in response to the boy's question "Are you one of the good guys?"
he answers in the affirmative.

"How do I know?" the boy asks.

"You don't," the man answers. "You'll just have to take a
shot."

The man seems kind, but seeming and being are two
very different things, as the boy now understands, even at his
young age. It is a world where people prey on each other and
it is difficult to accept the possibility of goodness. So he asks
another question, then another, then another:

Do you have a little boy?
We have a little boy and we have a little girl.
How old is he?
He's about your age. Maybe a little older.
And you didn't eat them.
No.
You don't eat people.

No. We don't eat people.
And I can go with you?
Yes. You can.
Okay then.
Okay.[70]

Even in the world of the Zombie Apocalypse, generosity is possible, and certainly in that world and in this, it is most necessary. Wherever people suffer, whenever people fear, only hospitality, peacemaking, and generosity can restore balance. We see our themes coming together here: community, our deepest humanity, and our highest ethical behavior are needed to close the door on our fear. Perhaps there are still zombies out there; perhaps other people want to do us harm, to take our goods, to take our lives. But goodness can still find us.

This doesn't happen in all of the zombie stories, of course. In some, hope is lost. In chapter 4 I'll explore the two possible futures and the two ways of seeing the world that are to be found in stories of the Zombie Apocalypse: nihilism and hope. As radically different as these outcomes may be, each has something to teach us, which should not surprise us by now. In a world turned upside down, we can see all that has gone bad. It takes nothing but awareness of the present horrors, whether zombies gathering outside or terrorists beheading people on the beach, to think that human history may end badly. But it will not perhaps surprise you by now that I hope for more, that I hope for hope, and that while some zombie tales most certainly point toward the dying of the light, I am most drawn to those that show the light extended and even rekindled.

AND IN THE END

Is the Zombie Apocalypse Good or Bad?

And I looked, and behold a pale horse: and his name
that sat on him was Death, and Hell followed with him.
And power was given unto them over the fourth part of
the earth, to kill with sword, and with hunger, and with
death, and with the beasts of the earth.

—REVELATION 6:8 (KJV)

Their world crumbled. The cities exploded. A whirlwind
of looting, a firestorm of fear. Men began to feed on men.

—MAD MAX 2: *The Road Warrior*

THE FILM *I AM LEGEND* opens with an interview with a scientist (Emma Thompson) who has discovered a viral cure for
cancer. *Oh no*, we think. Whenever humankind tries to cheat
death (or tamper in God's domain) we can be sure that some
sort of judgment is going to follow, and so it does here. We
cut from the interview with the scientist to the title "3 Years
Later" and the desolate streets of New York City. Wind whips
through the deserted city, deer and other animals have replaced human traffic, and cars sit unmoving as grass grows in
the streets. In this version of the story, Robert Neville is, so
far as we know, the last human being on earth, and each night
he must barricade himself in his brownstone against the
attacks of the virals who seek to kill him. As in the novel, he

is a man alone (although he at least begins the story with a dog), and what drives him is the hope that he will discover some cure for this virus and that he will find other living humans who have escaped destruction at the hands of the Nightwalkers.

The end of the world is here; fold in horror, action, disaster, or superhero narrative and stir. I have focused on stories of the Zombie Apocalypse—that is, apocalyptic and post-apocalyptic narratives about the survival of a small number of humans faced with the threat of annihilation at the hands of inhuman monsters who seek to eat or assimilate them. But you can't turn on the TV, go to a multiplex, or walk through a game store without being inundated with such apocalyptic narratives. The apocalypse story is one of the most repeated ones in human history, but stories of the end of the world have never been more popular than they are today.

Superhero comics would not be comics—at least in recent times—without the threat of world-ending villainy, cosmic disaster, or extraterrestrial invasion. While Superman, the original superhero, initially dealt with domestic violence, slumlords, and bank robbers (and such street-level crime remains an appropriate setting for heroes like Daredevil and Batman), the narrative stakes were raised by the escalating powers of Superman and such other characters as Green Lantern, the Fantastic Four, and Thor. Why have a Norse god of thunder and not have him wrestle with the coming doom that is called Ragnarok in the Norse legend of the end of the world? Why have a hero who can move planets and travel through time, like Superman, and never have him grapple with cosmic-level events that threaten whole worlds—or all that is? ("Nothing less than the end of all that is!" was a tagline of DC Comics' 1980s comic event *Crisis on Infinite Earths*, one of many examples of apocalyptic storytelling in comics of recent decades.)

Although street-level menaces were much closer to readers' actual experience, these stories of apocalypse were the ones that begged to be told and that people begged to read at the time when Marvel began to offer them, tales in which humanity faces the end of the world. Likewise in our superhero films, whether *Avengers, Guardians of the Galaxy*, or *Superman v. Batman: Dawn of Justice*, we see the coming of an alien menace that threatens everything. Without heroic intervention—and a substantial assist from luck, fate, or whatever Higher Power might be out there—it looks like the end.

But these are only the most recent iterations of an ancient narrative. Apocalyptic narratives go back to the earliest recorded human storytelling. We find a worldwide flood in the story of Noah and the Ark and in the earliest great literary work we know of, *The Epic of Gilgamesh*, and the Hebrew Bible, composed hundreds of years before the birth of Christ, offers an apocalyptic vision of a field of bones that come to life—a chilling vision that ultimately proves to be about hope:

> The hand of the LORD came upon me, and he brought me out by the spirit of the LORD and set me down in the middle of a valley; it was full of bones.
>
> He led me all around them; there were very many lying in the valley, and they were very dry.
>
> He said to me, "Mortal, can these bones live?" I answered, "O Lord GOD, you know."
>
> Then he said to me, "Prophesy to these bones, and say to them: O dry bones, hear the word of the LORD.
>
> Thus says the Lord GOD to these bones: I will cause breath to enter you, and you shall live.

I will lay sinews on you, and will cause flesh to come upon you, and cover you with skin, and put breath in you, and you shall live; and you shall know that I am the LORD."

So I prophesied as I had been commanded; and as I prophesied, suddenly there was a noise, a rattling, and the bones came together, bone to its bone.

I looked, and there were sinews on them, and flesh had come upon them, and skin had covered them; but there was no breath in them.

Then he said to me, "Prophesy to the breath, prophesy, mortal, and say to the breath: Thus says the LORD GOD: Come from the four winds, O breath, and breathe upon these slain, that they may live."

I prophesied as he commanded me, and the breath came into them, and they lived, and stood on their feet, a vast multitude.

Then he said to me, "Mortal, these bones are the whole house of Israel. They say, 'Our bones are dried up, and our hope is lost; we are cut off completely.'

Therefore prophesy, and say to them, Thus says the LORD GOD: I am going to open your graves, and bring you up from your graves, O my people; and I will bring you back to the land of Israel.

And you shall know that I am the LORD, when I open your graves, and bring you up from your graves, O my people.

I will put my spirit within you, and you shall live, and I will place you on your own soil; then you shall know that I, the LORD, have spoken and will act," says the LORD.[1]

Although the world is shaken by the events described, apocalypse represents a fundamental shift in the way the world works. It can work for good as well as ill. Note how God describes these dry bones as a missing part of the House of Israel—a people with no hope who need to be reconnected, to have the breath of God breathed back into them so that they can know real life. Or, in the story of Noah and the Flood, consider how the end of the world is a disaster beyond parallel, but the story concludes with God's promise never again to destroy the world by water, and one faithful man and his family survive to offer the world a chance to start anew, without the evil that so offended God in the first place. (Of course, this proves to be a vain hope, humans being as they are, but hope is hope all the same.)

It's probably useful to note here in this short history the distinction between apocalyptic story lines in literature and pop culture and the traditional literature that is called "apocalyptic." Although they are related and share some surface characteristics, they have different purposes and different outcomes. Daniel in the Hebrew Bible, the First and Second Books of Enoch, the Fourth Book of Ezra, and the Christian Testament's Book of Revelation diverge from our pop culture apocalyptic narratives in significant ways. In the secular stories, the human race faces the end of the world and either averts it or lives into it. The apocalyptic genre has historically had more of a cosmic and spiritual dimension. As James L. Kugel observes, in apocalyptic literature, an interpreter is given some "glimpse of divine secrets" and "the great and imminent conclusion" toward which history is headed.[2] Bart Ehrman defines apocalypse as a genre that reveals "the heavenly mysteries that can make sense of earthly realities."[3] Generally it is not about action but about revelation, not about conflict but about growing awareness. Apocalypse is a prediction of the future, a story that helps make sense of a sometimes difficult present.

Our current secular stories of the end of things may be less about hidden knowledge. They tend to depict an effort to prevent a predicted cataclysm or, more often in the context of this book, to prepare for and live through it. This world is coming to an end; a new world is coming. Such is the thrust of both our pop culture apocalyptic stories and the traditional literature of the apocalypse. In this chapter I will explore whether zombie narratives imagine this cataclysm to be a good thing or a bad thing.

The secular visions of the eschaton—the world to come, often arrived at through cataclysm or bloody struggle—that pervade our movies, TV, comics, games, and entire culture draw their settings and tensions from the long-standing tradition. In fact, our modern stories have in common their derivation from Christian apocalyptic thought. As John Gray writes in *Black Mass: Apocalyptic Religion and the Death of Utopia*, "visions of Apocalypse have haunted Western life" since Jesus and his followers promulgated a narrative about how "sickness and death, famine and hunger, war and oppression would all cease to exist after a world-shaking battle in which the forces of evil would be utterly destroyed."[4]

Even those who do not consider themselves followers of Christ or who may be proponents of a political system rather than a religious belief system (Gray's book, for example, explores apocalyptic leanings in regimes as different as Soviet Communism, Nazism, and the George W. Bush administration) find themselves retelling the Christian story of apocalypse and, in some sense, living into it. Their secular attempts to remake the world or prevent disaster are closely linked to religious attempts to predict, faithfully endure, or even benefit from the end of the world.

The most influential tale in this context is the Book of Revelation, the final book in the Christian Testament. The Revelation to John, as it is also sometimes called, or the Apocalypse, as it is named in the original Greek, has spawned innumerable fantasies, fears, and hopes and has become a meaning-making narrative for the West. As Jonathan Kirsch writes in a book with the grandiose but accurate subtitle *How the Most Controversial Book in the Bible Changed the Course of Western Civilization*, "Revelation is always present, sometimes in plain sight and sometimes just beneath the surface."[5] For two thousand years the apocalyptic ideas contained in Revelation have shaped the way we live, believe, vote, and are entertained, even if, as Raymond Brown and many other biblical scholars argue, they have done so for the wrong reasons. Some Christians have always taken the book as a reliable guide to the end of the world, believing that John, the purported author of the Revelation, received prophetic knowledge of the future that he shared in coded symbolic language. These Christians have believed that this secret knowledge could be a road map for the discerning, allowing them to anticipate—and even prepare for—the coming horror. Brown notes that many other Christians think that Revelation predicts the future only in the most general and faithful sense, a sense familiar from all the other apocalyptic literature. For these believers, Revelation has communicated "an absolute conviction that God would triumph by saving those who remained loyal and by defeating the forces of evil."[6] The details of this triumph—the exact date, place, and time—are not and cannot be known, but the triumph itself is not in doubt.

Because of this disagreement over how to read Revelation and what it actually contains, its status has always been somewhat suspect in the Christian church; Clement of Alexandria, Tertullian, and Irenaeus, among other early Christian sages, accepted Revelation as an authoritative Christian text, but it has also been marginalized by many from that time to ours.

Augustine, in *City of God*, argued that reading Revelation as a prediction of the future, as too many did, required believers to accept "ridiculous fancies."[7] Martin Luther included the book in his Bible, but he, Ulrich Zwingli, and John Calvin chose not to base their teachings on it. Calvin wrote commentaries on every canonical book in the Christian Testament *except* Revelation. It's a work that has been variously loved and feared and swept to one side.

In our time, Christians who oppose the futurist interpretations of biblical literalists have often scorned the book. Those who read Revelation as allegorical and historical are appalled by prophetic readings, and most scholars contend that to read Revelation as anything other than a pastoral letter dealing with historical events is to misread it.[8] Nonetheless, any discussion of the apocalyptic in the United States and in the West generally requires acknowledgment that these methods of misreading Revelation have filtered far and wide and have shaped the way we view the world—even if, we insist, this is not the way we view the world. Revelation continues to make its way into science fiction, fantasy, and horror stories about the end of the world, no matter what the faith of the storytellers. As Nicholas Guyatt has said, anyone watching movies or reading about the end of days will discover Revelation's influence.[9]

The Zombie Apocalypse can unfold in different ways. In one version, fate, God, hubris, or simply bad luck ushers in a cosmos-shaking event, which may be for good or ill, and the world changes. Here we can look to Romero's zombie films, the world of *The Walking Dead*, *Planet Terror*, or *Zombieland*. In these narratives the event has taken place, all social institutions have fallen, and the only questions are whether human beings will survive, and what that survival will do to them.

In other stories, even though there may be great struggle, humans manage to stave off the cataclysm and avert total destruction. Imagine here the stories told in *Shaun of the Dead*, *Scouts Guide to the Zombie Apocalypse*, or *The Zombie Survival Handbook*'s Class 1 or Class 2 outbreaks. At the end of these stories, although we and the characters involved have had a right good scare, some stability returns, and the old world or something like it is restored. Institutions have not been overthrown, cities are not deserted graveyards, and the event will become part of history in a world where history books will continue to be written and published. Here the story is about how humanity triumphed over death and destruction.

However the Zombie Apocalypse story gets told, our storytellers reflect either nihilism (a belief that life is essentially meaningless and nothing that humans do ultimately matters) or hope (a belief that despite death and suffering, life actually has meaning and purpose) in the ways they present their final outcomes. Will humanity be destroyed, leaving nothing to mark our passing? Think here of the endings of both versions of *Dawn of the Dead*, the hardly hopeful ending of the original where two survivors board a helicopter almost out of fuel, and the far less hopeful postcredits footage of the sequel, in which it seems clear that all the survivors have been destroyed or turned to undead. Consider also the ending of *28 Weeks Later*, where the Rage virus, once confined to England, has spread across the globe, and zombies are seen emerging into the streets of Paris. All is lost. But other stories wonder if this ending is The End. Will humanity experience some new birth, even if the apocalypse cannot be contained? Will individual humans be transformed by the powerful conflicts that come with this transition? Can the apocalypse ever be read as a positive thing, despite the horror and heartbreak it brings? Some stories suggest that all of these are possible.

Scholars have sometimes seen this distinction as determined by whether the imagined apocalypse has a religious dimension, that is, whether divine or other powerful beings have decreed the end of the world as part of their plan for the rescue of the cosmos. Daniel Wojcik has written that what we might call "religious apocalyptic" affirms "an orderly cosmos, the end of evil and suffering, the meaning of human life, and the millennial realm of peace and justice." Some nonreligious apocalypses also employ these hopeful tropes, but as Wojcik notes, secular stories of apocalypse are generally "devoid of the component of worldly redemption, and therefore tend to be characterized by a sense of hopelessness and despair."[10] Certainly many of our pop culture narratives of the end of the world evoke these emotions. But there is, as I've noted, the possibility for hope as well as despair. In some apocalyptic narratives, God, fate, or some other supernatural force sets the apocalypse into motion, "human beings endure," faithfully, as Adele Yarbo Collins puts it, and by tale's end the cosmos is somehow transformed. This is a sacred apocalypse, and horrific as its events might be, the end of the world works out for the best. In other apocalyptic narratives, human annihilation awaits if this cataclysm cannot be prevented or somehow overcome.[11]

So despair or determination, hopelessness or hope, are possible outcomes of the Zombie Apocalypse. Sometimes these contrasting narratives fight it out even within the covers of the same comic or the trailer of the same film: the apocalypse may be a given, but whether it will ultimately be for good or ill depends on the humans involved in it, and the way that we, its audience, receive it. But both narratives can be of use to us, and both visions help to explain the popularity of the zombie narrative. Whether we are impelled by tales of the end of the world to make changes in the current world or are encouraged to withstand our present difficulties by someone else's steadfast perseverance, good may ultimately emerge. Humankind may be stretched to its limits, tested to the end of its endurance. But thanks to our consumption of these stories, we too can rebound, can emerge stronger and more optimistic about a future that, presumably, does not include an actual Zombie Apocalypse.

EVERYTHING DIES: THE ZOMBIE APOCALYPSE AND NIHILISM

> Death is the only thing you can count on in this universe.
>
> —THE BLACK HAND, *DC's Blackest Night*

In the first chapter of Richard Matheson's *I Am Legend* (a key source for Romero's *Night of the Living Dead*, and thus the Alpha of all our zombie narratives), we meet Robert Neville. What we encounter in him is powerful loneliness. In the first chapter, after inspecting his home for the damage done during the night by the marauding undead, Neville knows that there are a number of things he ought to do for his health and sanity, but he doesn't, "for he was a man and he was alone and these things had no importance to him."[12] It is a portrait of abject hopelessness. Why does he go on living? Or is he merely breathing? So far as he knows, he is the last man on earth (the title of a 1964 film adaptation of *I Am Legend*), and even a dog would be such company for him that when he encounters one uninfected but terrified, he spends days trying to coax it into the house with him. In the end, Neville is captured by the undead, and at the close of the book, he takes poison. His sole comfort is that they seem as terrified of him, the great slayer of their kind, as he ever was of them. "I am legend," are the last words of the book, and then the last human is gone.[13] Death and destruction have won, and homo sapiens has vanished from the planet for all time.

In some stories, including *I Am Legend* and *Night of the Living Dead*, hope is dashed and meaning denied. The characters we have followed and with whom we have identified are killed or, worse, now number among the walking dead; whatever light they were carrying has gone out of the universe. In these versions of the Zombie Apocalypse, the cataclysm has no positive meaning, no cosmic redemption, and ultimately no survivors. Whether we have brought this disaster on ourselves, whether it has been worsened by our human greed or prejudice, or whether we are simple victims, in this story line the end of the world extinguishes all that was good about human life and leaves the human race in darkness.

In some of these tales of hopelessness, the apocalypse is explained by science. In the *I Am Legend* and *28 Days Later* mythos, for example, the monsters are created by a virus; in *Night of the Living Dead* a returning satellite is proposed as the cause of the dead walking; and gases with remarkable properties are responsible for the outbreaks in *Return of the Living Dead* and *Planet Terror*. Yet even in stories with scientific explanations of the apocalypse, myth and religion are often invoked to make sense of the doom that has befallen humankind. The preacher in Matheson's novel calls the undead wave a curse that people have brought on themselves by their own sin and failure to repent of it: "Do you want to come crawling back out of the grave like a monster out of hell?" the preacher asks. "Do you want to be turned into godless, night-cursed husks, into creatures of eternal damnation?"[14] Famously, in *Dawn of the Dead*, the plague is assigned a cosmic religious significance: "When there's no more room in Hell, the dead will walk the earth." However we explain the disaster, in these stories humankind is punished in some way: for sins or for pride or for overreaching. "He tampered in God's domain" was a much-repeated gag line from *Mystery Science Theater*, the cult favorite comedy show in which comedians mocked bad movies. It could be applied to many of these stories as well.

Romero's zombie films set this pattern of nihilism and hopelessness. In *Night of the Living Dead*, the bickering of the human characters as the undead menace closes in, the cowardice and inhumanity acted out by some of them, and the meaningless death of the hero leave a palpable mood of despair after the horror fades. In *Dawn of the Dead*, the human characters are largely destroyed by their human impulses toward acquisition and entertainment, and in *Day of the Dead* they are victims of their impulses toward violence, prejudice, and unethical behavior. Romero's films are exemplars of social criticism, and the failures of their human societies offer considerable insight into the failings of our own. As the Terminator (Arnold Schwarzenegger) says in another apocalyptic block-buster, *Terminator II: Judgment Day*, "it's in your nature to destroy yourselves." But perhaps by recognizing this nature, these tendencies toward self-destruction, we can stop short of the all-out apocalypse embodied in Romero's films.

Perhaps.

Although it takes place in the nineteenth-century American West and not in a postapocalyptic landscape like *The Road*, Cormac McCarthy's earlier novel *Blood Meridian: Or the*

Evening Redness in the West has the feel of the Zombie Apocalypse about it. It shows human nature descending into its most self-destructive tendencies. While *The Road* won the Pulitzer Prize and *All the Pretty Horses* the National Book Award, many critics call *Blood Meridian* McCarthy's greatest novel. Certainly it's one of the most difficult in its subject matter, an epic exploration of human darkness unleashed. The novel follows its protagonist, The Kid, a huge and frightening man called Judge Holden, and the Glanton gang as they ravage their way across the landscape, scalping, setting fires, "demanding drink and women."[15]

Rather than a symbol of possibility, as it is sometimes read, the American West here is the wasteland we've encountered before, a blasted landscape of death in which death walks, and these ravenous killers are like zombies, but worse because they have agency and choice. The book ends with the judge doing something to The Kid in an outhouse in Fort Griffin, Texas. In a book crammed with depictions of horrifying violence and depravity, this "something" is left undescribed. We see only the shock and horror of two men who open the outhouse door and encounter the aftermath. Critics debate whether the judge has killed the kid or "merely" raped him, but whatever his last appalling act has been, the judge, an almost supernaturally powerful figure of death and destruction, is left as the only figure standing—or, rather, dancing like some prehistoric figure around a cave fire, and proclaiming that he will never die. Reading *Blood Meridian* is like taking a bath in every monstrous thing humans would do if they could; it is as though Negan were the focus of *The Walking Dead* instead of Rick. The book leaves you feeling that in such a world, hope is impossible and darkness inescapable.

In *Blackest Night*, a 2009–2010 cross-title comic event from DC Comics, death breaks loose in the universe, and everyone who has ever cheated death is called to account. It features two major characters who question the value of life. Nekron, the Lord of the Unliving, is the most powerful dark force in the universe and the very embodiment of Death. His lieutenant is the Black Hand, a supervillain who believes that life is arbitrary and filled with chaos and should be replaced by the sweet equality of death: "Life favors some and ignores others. But our respective standings are irrelevant when it comes to death. In death, we are all equal. We are all silent and cold.... Inevitably, every living thing would've died, many in horrific ways after horrific lives. I'm saving them from years of misery and pain."[16] As the living die and the dead rise, including most of DC's stable of heroes, hope begins to fade. For the forces of death in the DC universe, the Blackest Night is about the cosmos returning to its proper course, a place in which death triumphs and life blinks out like a snuffed candle.

A primary appeal of the wildly popular *Marvel Zombies* narrative is the transgressive frisson of seeing good debased and heroes act like villains. As Iron Man, Spider-Man, Wolverine, the Fantastic Four, and other archetypal heroes become depraved cannibals, we as readers experience the tension of wanting them to be stopped and at the same time, wanting those characters we love to continue to exist in some fashion. In the opening arc of the Marvel Zombies story, the heroes take on a more morally ambiguous figure in the Marvel universe—Galactus, the Devourer of Worlds—and devour him. After assimilating his cosmic power, they take to the spaceways, consuming planet after planet. A more unhappy ending would be difficult to imagine; good has been corrupted by hunger, life is at the mercy of cosmic evil, and some of the brightest lights in existence have gone out. It is an ending that suggests that even in a universe with super-powered heroes, someday all we know and love will disappear.

28 Days Later takes us back into a world where hope retains a foothold despite the Zombie Apocalypse. At the end of the story a NATO jet flies over the remote cottage where Selena and Jim have taken refuge. Like the dove that returns to the Ark bearing an olive leaf in the story of Noah and the Flood, that jet suggests that life might still be possible some-where. Certainly *28 Weeks Later* begins with that hope. When NATO forces begin to reintroduce survivors into Britain twenty-eight weeks after the original infestation (when, it is thought, the original victims of the virus have starved), it looks as though the world might actually return to its origi-nal contours and all that brutality and violence will fade into painful memory. However, the virus lies dormant, and soon it has broken out again. The Rage sweeps through the new settlers and then spreads from Britain to the Continent. In the movie's final scene, virals pour out of the Paris Metro, with the iconic Eiffel Tower in the background. Like the clos-ing credits of the *Dawn of the Dead* remake, this is an ending that suggests that "The End" is truly The End.

In *The Walking Dead*, the trajectory likewise seems stead-ily downward so far as hope and human striving are con-cerned. Character after character has been eliminated at the hands of zombies or humans. In the finale of season 6, two of the members of Rick's community were beaten to death by Negan in front of the others. (At the time of this writing, no audience member including me was shown who those victims were!) For critic David Sims of the *Atlantic*, this death was the final straw: he has watched the show from its beginnings, suffered the deaths and tragedies year by year. But to be brought to the narrative point of knowing that someone presumably essential to the show has died, without even being told who that person was, felt to Sims as though the creators of this world were playing sadistic games with the audience. "We suffered through this whole season just to get beaten over the head," Sims opined, and his collaborator, Lenika Cruz, agreed that it was "deeply unfair to the viewer."[17]

They can kill whoever they want has long been a part of the implied contract for those of us who watch *The Walking Dead*, *Game of Thrones*, and other contemporary serial dramas. But for Sims and Cruz, the world of *The Walking Dead* had become too cynical, too nihilistic, too toxic to continue watching. This reaction is shared, of course, by others— many people have told me "I can't watch that" or "I had to stop watching," and I understand. My entry into Robert Kirkman's zombie universe was reading *The Walking Dead* comics, and I read up to the point where it began to feel to me as though I was being pulled into a dark cave with each additional character death. Where was the hope? I asked myself. Who was the moral exemplar that might rescue this story from ultimate darkness? And I could not answer. So I stopped reading the comic, and after viewing the first few episodes of the TV show when it first aired, I stopped watching it as well, only returning to it as I researched this book.

How these stories of the end make their consumers feel may help us define whether the moods they embody are primarily nihilistic or hopeful, and *The Walking Dead* has rarely made me feel hopeful. For every heartfelt and affirmative moment, like the reunion of Rick with his family or Daryl feeding Baby Judith, or Michonne and Rick forming a couple, there are a dozen moments of unexpected violence, unearned tragedy, and seemingly meaningless death. Several of the characters have actually argued this point for us: that theirs is a world without hope, full of savagery. Andrea tells Dale why she wanted to die at the CDC: "All I wanted after my sister died was to get out of this endless horrific nightmare." And after Carl is shot and is recovering on Hershel's farm, Lori wonders at length if it would be better for him to die than to come back into this world and end up "just another animal who doesn't know anything except to survive."

It can be argued—and indeed makes good structural narrative sense—that the joyful moments on the show or in the comic are that much more powerful emerging as they do from the miasma of negative emotion and hopelessness. Certainly, many critics continue to think of *The Walking Dead* as one of the most powerful shows on TV, and it continues to be the most popular TV show on the planet. Something about this storytelling has touched its audience.

But as we think about where the series is going and what the producers' endgame might be, it is hard to imagine that we are going to emerge in a sunlit vale resembling a Thomas Kinkade painting. I expect instead that the scene will be lit in grays and blacks, more resembling the late works Mark Rothko painted before he committed suicide (such as "Untitled/Black on Gray"), which critic Roberta Smith has described as "barren moonscapes," although I would be happy to be surprised.[18]

Finally, I think about the Call of Duty zombie modules, among the most popular zombie experiences on the planet. In them, gamers can gather with a group to fend off waves of zombies in a city, in a suburban setting, or in the trenches. They run, fight, hide, and try to survive, although winning is never a possibility. Successful players measure their accomplishment by the number of waves of zombies they've survived. But defeating the zombies is an impossibility. Eventually, no matter the player's skill, she or he will be defeated. It is a no-win scenario in which the zombies will always triumph.

Many of our stories of the Zombie Apocalypse are informed by despair, entropy, and nihilism. In films, games, and other narratives, it looks as though death is going to have the final say and light and life are passing out of the world. These impulses are fitting. We live in a world in which life often seems to be holding on by its fingernails and, as the poet Charles Sorley wrote during his own World War I apocalypse, "great death has made all his for evermore."[19] But as powerful and painful as many of our stories of the Zombie Apocalypse may be, others offer hope, whether in small character shifts or large cosmic movements. The dead may walk the earth, but the living survive—and even thrive.

This is not about whether you see the glass as half full or half empty. It's about whether you imagine that in the story to come, the glass will be emptied and possibly even shattered beyond future use—or that the glass might at some point be refilled with cold clear water or even with sparkling Veuve Cliquot. Our stories of the apocalypse are wrestling with the possibility of hope—is there any?—and our destiny, and they are shaped by how the artists see the world, what the world that story is mirroring looks and feels like. The world in 1340, or 1917, or 1968, or 2016 may very well be a world where it is difficult to see our race as on anything but a slow (or fast!) slide to ultimate destruction.

But even in stories in which the world ends, apocalyptic literature often offers up some version of hope, and sometimes the apocalypse is a central part of that hope; the world could never have gotten to the place it needed to be without a massive reboot. In the end, in the words of the medieval Christian saint Julian of Norwich, despite all that has passed, all will be well, and all will be well, and all manner of things will be well.

ALL WILL BE WELL: A LITTLE APOCALYPSE CAN BE A GOOD THING

—I'm glad that the end of the world is working out for someone.

JON SNOW, "Mother's Mercy," *Game of Thrones*

On the surface of it, the coming of the apocalypse seems to be nothing but negative. As a story, it is an acknowledgment that things are going wrong for the world in which we live. At the opening of the film *Gravity*, astronaut Matt Kowalsky (George Clooney) says, for the first of many times, "Houston, I have a bad feeling about this mission." Following as closely as it does on a title that reads "Life is impossible in space," we are inclined to give that premonition some weight.

> Yes, it's the end of the world.
> Yes, life is impossible.
> We know that full well.

We're a decade and a half on from September 11, 2001, but we saw the planes crash, we saw the towers burn and fall, and we saw the world's greatest superpower reduced to the status of victim. In the years since, we've seen the nations of the world spend over a trillion dollars in the war on terror, seen our patterns and our habits change so that in some ways our old lives are no longer recognizable, and seen the ethical compromises that we and our leaders agreed to because we feared the end of the world. And still terrorists blow themselves up in marketplaces, attack trains and theaters and stadiums and churches, and threaten to do much worse to us if they can.

And that's to say nothing of ecological degradation, the melting polar ice caps, rising sea levels, the death of bees, the spread of new diseases, instability in the financial markets, the rise of incivility in our political discourse.

Yes, I'll stop there.

Things are bad. But having some historical perspective— and realizing that the present is not the first time that the dead have gotten up and walked around—reminds us that often in human history people have perceived what they thought would be the end of the world. Death was ascendant, the species was on its way out, we might as well get our heads around it—yet we survived.

We are still here. That doesn't mean we aren't still apprehensive about all of these threats, that they aren't, many of them, genuine threats, and that we shouldn't admit that things look bad.

In these stories about the Zombie Apocalypse, though, even the ones where there seems to be little or no hope, we are offering an essentially optimistic narrative act. By admitting that things are bad, by sharing our dread, and by allowing ourselves to mutually agree that we are all a part of this alarming reality, we are at least taking away the suffering experienced by Robert Neville in his solitude. We are not alone, for others suffer alongside us.

In his essay "The Man on the Train," novelist Walker Percy tells a story about a lonely man who is miserable in his life and riding a commuter train into work. This is horrible solitude. He is trapped in his own misery, alone in his awareness that the world is not going well. On the same train, there is another unhappy man, who happens to be reading a story about an unhappy man on a train. The difference is striking. Yes, this second man says. This is exactly how it feels. Someone understands what I'm seeing and feeling. The world is a mess. But at least I'm not alone in knowing it, seeing it, and feeling it.

As Percy put it, "the nonreading commuter exists in true alienation, which is unspeakable; the reading commuter rejoices in the speakability of his alienation and in the new triple alliance of himself, the alienated character, and the author. His mood is affirmatory and glad: Yes! That is how it is!—which is an aesthetic reversal of alienation."[20] Telling the truth—that the world seems to be falling apart—allows readers and audiences to know that they are accompanied in their own experiences, that however they might feel in the moment, they are not alone, even when times are tough.

Does it feel like the end of the world to you?

Yes! Me too, sometimes.

See how that works? The simple act of telling a story about the end of the world is in itself an affirmative act, no matter how bleak the story. But in some of these stories, much more happens: in some of them, the characters—and through them, the world itself—are rescued and restored. We've already seen that one of the religious ideas of the apocalyptic is that things are bad, but if we are faithful, we will live into that new world where all will be put right. It is this notion behind the Book of Revelation, which has so frightened so many over the last 2000 years, to which I call your attention. Despite the fact that the world is ending, hope is ascendant. John the Revelator hears that the world is in the process of becoming the Kingdom of God:

Then the seventh angel blew his trumpet, and there were loud voices in heaven, saying,

> "*The kingdom of the world has become the kingdom of our Lord*
> *and of his Messiah,*
> *and he will reign forever and ever.*"

Then the twenty-four elders who sit on their thrones before God fell on their faces and worshiped God, singing,

> "*We give you thanks, Lord God Almighty,*
> *who are and who were,*
> *for you have taken your great power*
> *and begun to reign.*
> *The nations raged,*
> *but your wrath has come,*
> *and the time for judging the dead,*
> *for rewarding your servants, the prophets*
> *and saints and all who fear your name,*
> *both small and great,*
> *and for destroying those who destroy the earth.*"

Then God's temple in heaven was opened, and the ark of his covenant was seen within his temple; and there were flashes of lightning, rumblings, peals of thunder, an earthquake, and heavy hail.

A great portent appeared in heaven: a woman clothed with the sun, with the moon under her feet, and on her head a crown of twelve stars.

She was pregnant and was crying out in birthpangs, in the agony of giving birth.[21]

It's the end of the world; it's also new birth. Travis Langley argues that one of the things the apocalyptic narrative offers us is the opportunity for "a worldwide do-over."[22] Out of this brokenness, out of this disaster, yes, even out of the end of the world, something good is coming. Many times when we think of apocalypse, we think only of death and destruction; we see only the zombies. But apocalypse also suggests the opportunity for new beginnings. J. R. R. Tolkien, who wrote with some creativity about apocalyptic things like dragon attacks and dark lords ascendant, wrote in an essay on fairy tales about the "good catastrophe."

Can there be such a thing? Well, on one level, if you are one of those characters eaten by zombies, crushed by the humanity trying to board the last train to safety, or starving on the road in the postapocalyptic world, clearly no, the apocalypse doesn't seem like such a good thing to you. On an individual basis, the *eucatastrophe* is often just a plain old disaster. However, at other times, individuals and even the larger world not only survive but thrive because of the challenging conditions, and this is a story we need to hear, living as we do in our own catastrophic times. "The eucatastrophic tale," Tolkien said, is the truest fairy tale, and in it we see "its highest function."[23] In a tale where we come to the point of disaster—and then see that disaster somehow miraculously or magically reversed, or see characters change, grow, and mature because of it—we are brought to believe that such reversals are possible, right, and just.

We are taught to see the world through the lens of hope.

By the time the characters have reached *The Walking Dead* season 2 episode "Cherokee Rose," many things have gone wrong. Not only have they lost several members of their community, but their hope in a governmental rescue dies at the Centers for Disease Control, and now one of their children, Sophia, has gone missing following a zombie attack. Daryl brings a flower to Carol, the grieving mother, and in the midst of their own apocalypse, he tells a story about another flower:

> The story is, when American soldiers were moving Indians off their land on the Trail of Tears, the Cherokee mothers were grieving and crying so much 'cos they were losing their little ones along the way: exposure, disease, starvation. A lot of 'em just disappeared. So the elders they said a prayer. Asked for a sign to uplift the mothers' spirits. Give 'em strength. Hope. The next day, this rose started to grow, right where the mothers' tears fell.
>
> I'm not fool enough to think there's any flowers blooming for my brother. But I believe this one bloomed for your little girl.

In the darkest night, a light shines. At the moment of greatest hopelessness, hope and beauty are still possible. And here the story—and the flower—are borne by an unlikely messenger. Daryl, who earlier has said that he works best alone, demonstrates compassion. He shows that he is capable of evolving. This character development is one of many positive things brought about by the apocalypse.

In *Blackest Night*, one of the bleakest comic events ever— has there ever been a starker or more terrifying few pages than the ones in which Superman, Wonder Woman, Green Arrow, and Superboy are transformed into members of the living dead?—death walks the earth, and the light of the universe appears to be on the verge of dying. But the Flash arrives on the scene with revivified heroes, and as he does, he speaks the words of Julian of Norwich: "All will be well."[24]

More pertinent, perhaps, even than these words (which are repeated throughout the *Blackest Night* graphic novel), are other words from Julian of Norwich. Although she lived at Ground Zero of the Black Plague (Norwich lost something like 75 percent of its population to the disease), although she experienced all the uncertainty and instability we said marked the Middle Ages, she had this vision that all would be well, that humanity would not only survive, but thrive. The final message she received from God, which came "with very great certainty, referring to all of us," is this: "You shall not be overcome."[25]

Although the world is filled with violence, chaos, and uncertainty, human striving continues to matter. All human beings are not overcome, and in many of our stories, characters become something new and better as a result of the Zombie Apocalypse. Francine in *Dawn of the Dead* learns to fly. In *Zombieland*, Columbus, crushed by his own anxieties and neuroses, learns to love, to accept friendship, and to be brave. Shaun, who had been like one of the dead, comes to life and loves Liz as she deserves, and if he still plays the occasional video game with Zombie Ed, at least we see that it isn't the entirety of who he now is. In *The Walking Dead*, Rick Grimes (although his ultimate fate remains a mystery to readers and viewers) becomes a leader and a warrior, a far cry from the small-town deputy we met at the beginning of his story. Daryl Davis has become a compassionate soul who loves his community. Michonne learns to accept love again. On and on and on, the roll call of Zombie Apocalypse victories, both large and small, resounds.

It is in our nature to destroy ourselves. Death may be on the ascendant. Humanity may seem to be on the ropes. The living dead may outnumber the living. But in many of our stories of the Zombie Apocalypse, we discover something like the reboot postulated by Professor Langley: humankind rising from the ashes of our culture and creating something new and beautiful. The Zombie Apocalypse can also be a transition to a great future for humankind as well as a catalyst for individual humans. Evan Calder-Williams, who writes that "an apocalypse is an end with revelation, a lifting of the veil," sees the apocalyptic not as a death to be mourned but as a rebuilding and rediscovering of what has been veiled by habit or history.[26] In this vision, life after the apocalypse is not so much about restoring things to the way they were, many of those ways flawed by consumerism, selfishness, prejudice, classism, and other human and institutional vanities, as it is about renewing the planet, about, in his words, "redrawing the maps and battle lines of the world."[27]

In the Song of Ice and Fire saga, Jon Snow, a bastard son of someone important who is now dead, rises through the ranks of the Night's Watch as the menace of the living dead and the White Walkers looms. He is one of the first to perceive the centrality of this threat to all humankind, one of the few to kill a wight in combat, one of the only humans to destroy a White Walker. He is voted Lord Commander of the Night's Watch and, pushing past the fear and prejudice of his men, saves the lives of thousands of Wildlings from north of the Wall, preserving them as well as preventing them from swelling the army of the dead. To be sure, his men reward this act with deceit and murder, but even here the universe is not through with Jon Snow; unlike the dead raised by the White Walkers, he is raised to new life, with freedom now to lead in the great final battle of life against death.

The eucatastrophe, then, is good flowing out of the disaster that ended the old world. Perhaps that good is physical, perhaps it is cultural, perhaps it is something else. But in coming back to the metaphor of the glass half-filled, we begin to see that what may emerge from the eucatastrophe is hope.

Four Quartets is a late poem by T. S. Eliot. I've discussed how his poem The Wasteland captured the fear of the end of the world inspired by World War I and trench warfare, that seeming triumph of death. Only two decades later, in the midst of World War II, Eliot was again looking at the end of the world. Even as bombs were falling on London, he wrote poems of possibility amid the madness. The sequence concludes with a poem called "Little Gidding," and with very pertinent wisdom; after quoting Julian of Norwich, Eliot opines that the end of our journey will be to arrive where we began, and to know the place for the very first time. The journey, in other words, may be fraught with danger, but it is a voyage into knowledge about ourselves and about the cosmos, and it carries us somewhere.

It is a journey that we have to take if we are to achieve true knowledge.

In one respect, the film version of I Am Legend ends tragically. Robert Neville, with whom we have spent the entire film, commits suicide, blowing up a laboratory full of Nightwalkers in his passing. But although for us as viewers this is tragic, the movie nonetheless ends with hope. Mark Protosevich told me that the crux of the conflict for him was figuring out why Neville doesn't give up:

> The key questions for such a character are, Why go on? Why not kill yourself? What's the point of living? Yes, there's a basic human desire to survive, but in these worlds we're talking about, there's not much to live for. So what would drive a person to do all he/she can to survive?
>
> For me, in I Am Legend, it was hope. He never gave up hope that there might be other survivors somewhere in the world. That was more important than "trying to find a cure" for the virus.[28]

Neville, who has been lost and alone, who has reached the point of despair when his dog Max dies, has fulfilled both of the goals that have occupied him: he has isolated a vaccine for the KV virus and, more important, he has discovered that there are other humans left. He is not alone. Although he dies, he does so knowing that human life will continue. Even at the close of his painful journey, he finds hope renewed.

In a previous book, *Entertaining Judgment*, one of my great discoveries was how many of our narratives employ the story structure of the Christian concept of Purgatory: in works from ancient times to our own, characters (and audiences) go through difficult, even harrowing experiences on their way to becoming new and more enlightened beings. "It's gotta be like this I know," sing Imagine Dragons in their 2015 hit "Roots"; "Hell has gotta come before you grow." It is the journey through the landscape of death that leads to wisdom. At the conclusion of Manuel Gonzales's "Escape from the Mall," Cowboy, our protagonist, sums up what the Zombie Apocalypse has meant to him—and what it might mean for us:

> And then I'm running, exhilarated by what I have just done, by what this might mean for me—not just escape from the mall, but a kind of escape from life, from my old life, from that tired old existence.
>
> I think to myself, *This was for the best. All of this.*
>
> And maybe I should feel worse for Roger and the security guard and the rest of the human race, but I can't help but wonder that maybe we need these kinds of moments. Not moments of quiet, but moments when our lives are upended by violent tragedy, monsters, zombies, because without them, how would we meet the men and women of our dreams, how would we make up for the sins of our pasts, how

would we show our true natures—brave, caring, strong, intelligent?

I wonder, How would we?[29]

In these stories of the apocalypse, happy endings are possible. That doesn't mean that people haven't died, or that horrible things haven't been done. But what it does mean is that those humans who populate the world and maybe the world itself are different, better, even, because of what has been endured. It means that in the great battle between life and death, the only war that matters, we continue to choose life, life in all its complications, with all its pain, with all its suffering, with all its unfairness.

The message of these stories of the Zombie Apocalypse is that in a world marked by fear and violence—a world very much like our own—we can still choose to live, and choose how to live. And in that choosing, you can make a difference.

You will not be overcome.

Light up the darkness.

CONCLUSION

Living with the Living Dead

Everything's going to be all right.

CARL GRIMES, "Internment," *The Walking Dead*

EVERY BOOK GROWS IN THE WRITING of it. When my editor and I first talked about this project in 2013, I was deep in the reading and writing for *Entertaining Judgment*, a book on our narratives of the afterlife and how we use them, and all I really knew was that I had a whole lot more material about the undead than I could possibly fit in that book. In the process of writing two formal proposals, of responding to the comments and criticism of readers, and of beginning to turn my attention solely to this topic, the book grew and grew, springing up, as books do, from seed to seedling, to, I hope, full-grown tree.

When I began the book, I wanted to find answers to the question I was regularly being asked, particularly by people over 40: Why are zombies so popular? I wanted to do justice to that question by considering it from a multitude of angles, deploying critical, cultural, psychological, spiritual, philosophical, political, and theological lenses. During the process of this exploration, I discovered much more than I expected. Instead of being purely a post-9/11 phenomenon, as I had originally imagined, it turned out that zombies are only the latest version of an artistic and narrative response to crisis that goes back 600 years or more. Discovering that the dead have walked the earth before 1968, and certainly before 2016, offered me a final insight into why it is we love these stories, and why they continue to be some of the most popular stories we tell.

The continued popularity of *The Walking Dead* and *Game of Thrones*, the endless hunger for zombie games, the books and graphic novels, and the seemingly unstoppable flood of straight-to-video zombie films and multimillion dollar Zombie Apocalypse blockbusters all testify to the troubled times in which we live, and to our desire to make some sense of our experience by consuming narratives about times even more troubled than ours. Jon Russo, co-creator of the Romero Zombie, writes that *The Walking Dead* is such a phenomenon today because it depicts how "all kinds of people in all kinds of circumstances must deal with the devastation, the destruction, the almost overpowering threat to their humanity."[1] But, as we've discovered, the appeal of *The Walking Dead*—and of all stories about the living dead—comes from the fact that all of us must deal with devastation, with destruction, with threats to our humanity.

In stepping into the world of the living dead, we are entertained, we are horrified, and, if we're not very careful, we are enlightened. We discover that it is okay to be a hero; we discover that we need each other to survive; we discover that sometimes, as hard as it may be, we are called to do the right thing, no matter the cost. We discover that although human nature may be in some way fallen and the universe unfeeling, our tomorrows could yet in some way be brighter than our today. Those meanings may be buried in gore and intestines, may be masked by the outstretched hands grasping in our direction. But if you've come this far in our journey together, I trust it is because you too recognize that the meanings are real, that whether you describe yourself as a zombie fanatic or as zombie-phobic, these are stories that matter, not just because millions of other people consume them, but because they offer an ongoing narrative way of understanding the world as it is.

So the next time you watch, or read, or play, or portray a zombie, pay close attention.

The living dead have something to tell you, and it may just save your life.

ACKNOWLEDGMENTS

As with much of my writing, I've been given substantial resources over a period of years for this project, and it would be criminal not to thank and recognize the people and institutions who have helped bring this book into being. First and foremost, I am grateful to the publishing professionals at Oxford University Press who had a vision for a second book reading culture for ultimate meanings, and who helped shepherd this book into being. I am graced with a great editor, Cynthia Read, with wonderful production help from Marcela Maxfield, Gwen Colvin, and Cameron Donahue, and have worked with phenomenal promotional folks in the United States (Cat Boyd, Lauren Jackson, Alyssa Russell, and Sara Levine) and in the United Kingdom (Katie Stileman and Rachel May). I am also grateful for the honest and thoughtful comments of the anonymous readers of the original proposal, who suggested important directions this finished book might take.

Baylor University supported the research and writing of this book with a research leave and with two grants from the

University Research Committee, one on post-9/11 literature
and culture and one on death in art and culture. My college,
led by Dean Lee Nordt, and my department, where I have
been supported by past chair Dianna Vitanza and current
chair Kevin Gardner, have offered support, encouragement,
and appreciation for the work I do as cultural critic and narrative theologian. My Baylor colleagues, particularly Hulitt
Gloer, Tom Hanks, Richard Russell, Carey Newman, and
Deanna Toten-Beard, talked with me about story, structure,
history, and theology and offered constant encouragement
on what was one of my most difficult books to write. I'm also
indebted to my students, both graduate and undergraduate,
particularly Sarah Tharp, who toiled as my research assistant
in the early phases of this project and helped to develop the
theory that zombies are merely the latest manifestation of the
living dead.

Much of this book was conceived, researched, and written in residence at Gladstone's Library in Hawarden, Wales,
where I have found a home and a writing haven over the past
seven years. Thanks to the Reverend Peter Francis, warden,
for the opportunity to write and be in residence, to Chef Alan
Hurst and all the staff for their hospitality, and to all those
guests I've met at the Library who have helped me write through
our conversations about narrative, culture, and religion.

On two occasions in the thinking and early writing stages,
I was hosted by the American Cathedral in Paris, whose dean,
the Very Reverend Lucinda Laird, has been a friend and
advocate for my work. I am grateful to her and to that community for conversations and research that shaped the final
product. During the planning and writing of this book, I was
also invited to speak at the American Library in Paris, where
I was hosted by Charlie Trueheart and Grant Rosenberg, at

Magdalene College, Cambridge, where my host was Rowan Williams, and at Kings College, London, where I was hosted by Tim Ditchfield, Russell Goulbourne, and Richard Burridge. Important questions about zombies and theology were asked at each of those talks, and many of my provisional answers were expanded into sections of this text.

At the Imperial War Museum in London, art curator Alexandra Walton set up my viewing of works from World War I, World War II, and the Holocaust. Alex also made herself available to answer questions via e-mail, for which I am grateful. While I did not work with curators at the British Museum or at the Louvre, my time spent at each great institution over the past few years informed this book.

My initial research on the apocalypse and popular culture was done several years ago at the Millennium Studies Center at Liverpool Hope University in Liverpool, England, where I was invited by John Walliss to deliver the Hope Theological Lecture and later returned on a research fellowship to use the collections. An earlier version of some of my conclusions on the apocalypse appeared in the article " 'Now the Whole World Stands on the Brink': Apocalypse and Eschatological Hope in Contemporary Superhero Comics," which appeared in the collection *The End Will Be Graphic: Apocalyptic in Comic Books and Graphic Novels* and was edited by my friend and frequent collaborator Dan W. Clanton, Jr.

I continue to be supported in my writing and my work exploring religion and culture by the Episcopal Seminary of the Southwest in Austin, where I office and enjoy the benefit of conversation with theologians, ethicists, Bible scholars, and counselors such as Scott Bader-Saye, Tony Baker, Cynthia Briggs-Kittredge, Gena Minnix, Jane Patterson, and

Steve Bishop. It is a continuing pleasure to be supported by this institution that had such impact on me.

Austin Film Festival Creative Director Erin Hallagan knew that I was writing a book reflecting on zombies, and she scheduled me to moderate a session on zombies in film and TV at the 2015 festival. There I had the chance to first make the acquaintance of writers Angela Kang and Mark Protosevich and to ask some questions that informed the book. Erin and Festival Director Barbara Morgan also made available to me transcripts of other panels on zombie films and TV, giving me access to information unique to the festival, which is one of America's great resources on story, craft, and structure.

Other friends, including Martyn Percy, Ken Malcolm, David Andrews, Greg Rickel, Sarah Bird, Owen Egerton, Donna Johnson, and many others talked with me about this project, encouraged me in my writing life, or otherwise helped in tangible and not so tangible ways. I am blessed in the quality of my friendships and of my friends.

Most particularly, during what I like to think of as "crunch time," the period in every writer's life when the ideas that have been floating around upstairs must at last be put on paper in more or less thoughtful and artful fashion, Terry Nathan generously offered me the use of his lake house in Kingsland, Texas, for several weeks. Without Terry's help, this book would have been impossible to complete, and the book's dedication is merely recognition of that fact. As hard as it was to think about zombies all day, I will always have fond memories of typing on the porch as the rain clattered off the tin roof and made rings in the lake, a beautiful contrast to my often challenging subject matter.

My son, Chandler Garrett, was an encouragement in the writing of this book, often intentionally. His expertise in games, movies, and TV made him a walking reference book for me, as well as an anecdotal example of how widespread the zombie narrative is in our culture. If ever I wondered if this book was worth writing, I had only to look at all the ways zombies were a part of my son's life, and I had my answer. Thanks, Bud.

My daughters, Lily and Sophie, know next to nothing about zombies except that they are walking dead people, and I am fine with their continued ignorance, at least for the present. My wife, Jeanie, my greatest treasure, my greatest fan, and my biggest support, also knows almost nothing about zombies, but she knows I am a writer who wants to understand things and help others to understand things, and she helped me carve out the time and space to write this book—and helped to build the home I will always want to return to when I'm done.

My thanks to all of these, and to you, Dear Reader, for your presence and participation in this conversation. May your journey through the zombie wastelands bring you, at last, to home.

Grace and peace—
Greg Garrett
Pentecost, 2016
Austin, Texas

NOTES

Introduction

1. Max Brooks, *The Zombie Survival Guide: Complete Protection from the Living Dead* (New York: Broadway, 2003), 154.
2. Spencer Kornhaber, Christopher Orr, and Amy Sullivan, "*Game of Thrones*: The Only War That Matters," *Atlantic*, June 1, 2015, http://www.theatlantic.com/entertainment/archive/2015/06/game-of-thrones-season-5-episode-8-roundtable-hardhome/394544/.
3. Angela Kang and Mark Protosevich (panelists), "Zombies and the Undead," Austin Film Festival, October 30, 2015.
4. Michael O'Sullivan, "'Dead' and Loving It," *Washington Post*, March 19, 2004, http://www.washingtonpost.com/wp-dyn/content/article/2004/03/19/AR2005033115788.html.
5. Roger Ebert, "Night of the Living Dead," rogerebert.com, January 5, 1969, http://www.rogerebert.com/reviews/the-night-of-the-living-dead-1968.
6. Jeffrey Goldberg, J. J. Gould, and Scott Meslow, "'The Walking Dead,' Like All Zombie Stories:...Not about Zombies at All," *Atlantic*, November 25, 2012, http://www.theatlantic.com/entertainment/archive/2012/11/the-walking-dead-like-all-zombie-stories-not-about-zombies-at-all/265549/.

7. Kim Paffenroth, *Gospel of the Living Dead: George Romero's Visions of Hell on Earth* (Waco, TX: Baylor University Press, 2006), 7–8.

8. Masahiro Mori, "The Uncanny Valley" (1970), trans. Karl F. MacDorman and Norri Kageki, *IEEE Spectrum*, June 12, 2012, http://spectrum.ieee.org/automaton/robotics/humanoids/the-uncanny-valley.

9. Norri Kageki, "An Uncanny Mind: Masahiro Mori on the Uncanny Valley and Beyond," *IEEE Spectrum*, June 12, 2012, http://spectrum.ieee.org/automaton/robotics/humanoids/an-uncanny-mind-masahiro-mori-on-the-uncanny-valley.

10. Travis Langley, "Introduction: The Uncanny Valley of the Shadow of Death," in *The Walking Dead Psychology: Psych of the Living Dead*, ed. Travis Langley (New York: Sterling, 2015), 4.

11. Paffenroth, *Gospel of the Living Dead*, 2, 17–22.

12. Chuck Klosterman, "My Zombie, Myself: Why Modern Life Feels Rather Undead," *New York Times*, December 10, 2010, http://www.nytimes.com/2010/12/05/arts/television/05zombies.html?pagewanted=all&_r=0.

13. Aleksandar Hemon, *The Making of Zombie Wars* (New York: Farrar, Straus and Giroux, 2015), 279–280.

14. Lydia Kiesling, "Aleksandar Hemon on Zombie Culture: 'America Deeply Believes in Violence,'" *Guardian*, May 7, 2015, https://www.theguardian.com/books/2015/may/07/aleksandar-hemon-the-making-of-zombie-wars-interview.

15. Dan Solomon, "Robert Kirkman: Geek Culture Rules," *SXSWorld*, November 2014, 12.

16. "Zombies at the Gates," *Economist*, March 23, 2013, 80; Gabriel Wildau, "China Bankruptcies Surge as Government Targets Zombie Enterprises," *Financial Times*, June 22, 2016, https://next.ft.com/content/70aec7b2-3869-11e6-a780-b48ed7b6126f.

17. Bryan Lowry, "Brownback Signs 'Zombie Preparedness Month' Proclamation," *Wichita Eagle*, September 30, 2015, http://www.kansas.com/news/politics-government/article37056684.html.

18. Centers for Disease Control, "Preparedness 101: Zombie Pandemic," July 16, 2012, http://www.cdc.gov/phpr/zombies/#/page/1; Michael Cieply, "A Risk for Films That Move at a Zombie's Pace," *New York Times*, March 18, 2013, http://www

.nytimes.com/2013/03/19/movies/zombie-and-other-genre-films-often-require-years-to-make.html?pagewanted=all&_r=0.

19. Evan Calder-Williams, *Combined and Uneven Apocalypse: Luciferian Marxism* (Winchester, England: Zero Books, 2010), 72.

20. Facebook message, March 22, 2013.

21. Karen Armstrong, *Jerusalem: One City, Three Faiths* (New York: Knopf, 1996), xviii; Eugene Thacker, *In the Dust of This Planet*, vol. 1 of *Horror of Philosophy* (Winchester, England: Zero Books, 2011), 2.

22. Alain de Botton, *Religion for Atheists: A Non-believer's Guide to the Uses of Religion* (New York: Pantheon, 2012), 12.

23. Romero's revision of the zombie story also moved us away from a concern for the zombies—in the Caribbean, victims who symbolize slave labor and exploitation—and toward a concern for the survivors who are menaced by zombies.

24. Christopher McKittrick, "Alex Garland on Screenwriting," *Creative Screenwriting*, January 6, 2016, http://creativescreen writing.com/alex-garland-on-screenwriting/.

25. Paffenroth, *Gospel of the Living Dead*, 34.

26. W. B. Yeats, "The Second Coming," in *Scanning the Century: The Penguin Book of the Twentieth Century in Poetry*, ed. Peter Forbes (London: Penguin, 1999), 54–55.

27. "What's Up with the Zombie Apocalypse?," *Straight Dope*, March 22, 2013, http://www.straightdope.com/columns/read/3098/what-s-up-with-the-zombie-apocalypse.

28. Erica E. Phillips, "Zombie Studies Gain Ground on College Campuses," *Wall Street Journal*, March 3, 2013, http://www.wsj.com/articles/SB100014240527023048511045793614519513 84512.

29. Andrew Bergman, *We're in the Money: Depression America and Its Films* (Chicago: Ivan R. Dee, 1992).

30. Daniel W. Drezner, "Metaphor of the Living Dead: Or, the Effect of the Zombie Apocalypse on Public Policy Discourse," *Social Research* 81.4 (2014), 825.

31. Lenika Cruz, personal e-mail, June 9, 2016.

32. Max Brooks, "A Conversation with Max Brooks," website of Max Brooks, http://www.maxbrookszombieworld.com/.

33. Roger Ebert, "The Dark Knight," RogerEbert.com, July 16, 2008, http://www.rogerebert.com/reviews/the-dark-knight-2008; John Anderson, "*The Hunger Games* Were Rigged," *Time*, November 20–December 7, 2015, http://time.com/4119956/hunger-games-rigged/?iid=sr-link1.

34. Clive Marsh, "On Dealing with What Films Actually Do to People: The Practice and Theory of Film Watching in Theology/Religion and Film," in *Reframing Theology and Film: New Focus for an Emerging Discipline*, ed. Robert K. Johnson (Grand Rapids, MI: Baker, 2007), 155.

35. Diane Winston, introduction to *Small Screen, Big Picture: Television and Lived Religion*, ed. Diane Winston (Waco, TX: Baylor University Press, 2009), 6.

36. "Zombies, Apes, and Vampires: Breathing New Life into Old Genres," Austin Film Festival, October 22, 2011.

37. Thacker, *In the Dust of This Planet*, 1.

38. *The Dead Will Walk*, dir. Perry Martin, Anchor Bay Entertainment, 2004.

39. *The Walking Dead*, vol. 1 (Berkeley: Image Comics, 2013), n.p.

40. Dalton Ross, "The Originals," *Entertainment Weekly*, February 19/26, 2016, 52.

41. Robert Kirkman, introduction to *Walking Dead*, vol. 1, n.p.

42. William Shakespeare, *Hamlet* 3.1.78–79.

43. Lesley Goldberg, "*The Walking Dead*'s Robert Kirkman on the Casting of Danai Gurira as Michonne," *Hollywood Reporter*, March 19, 2012, http://www.hollywoodreporter.com/live-feed/walking-dead-robert-kirkman-danai-gurira-michonne-casting-301729.

44. "A Day on Set with Norman Reedus," *Entertainment Weekly*, February 13, 2015, 31.

45. *Walking Dead*, vol. 1, n.p.

46. Raina Kelley, "The Social Significance of Zombies," *Newsweek*, October 29, 2010, http://www.newsweek.com/social-significance-zombies-221328.

47. Stephen Marche, "Why Zombies Are Everywhere Now," *Esquire*, June 19, 2013, http://www.esquire.com/entertainment/movies/a23139/why-zombies-are-everywhere/.

48. John Casey, *After Lives: A Guide to Heaven, Hell, and Purgatory* (Oxford: Oxford University Press, 2009), 14.

49. Moira Macdonald, "'Shaun of the Dead': From Pink-Skinned Loser to Heroic Zombie Chaser," *Seattle Times,* September 23, 2004, http://community.seattletimes.nwsource.com/archive/?slug=shaun24&date=20040923.
50. Calder-Williams, *Combined and Uneven Apocalypse,* 102–103.

Chapter 1

1. Evelyn Lamb, "Zombie Fever: A Mathematician Studies a Pop Culture Epidemic," *Scientific American,* October 30, 2013, http://blogs.scientificamerican.com/roots-of-unity/zombie-fever-a-mathematician-studies-a-pop-culture-epidemic/.
2. Manuel Gonzales, "Escape from the Mall," in *The Miniature Wife and Other Stories* (New York: Riverhead, 2013), 285.
3. Sarah Lawson, "An Open Letter to the White Walker Army," *New Yorker,* June 11, 2015, http://www.newyorker.com/culture/sarah-larson/an-open-letter-to-the-white-walker-army.
4. John Casey, *After Lives: A Guide to Heaven, Hell, and Purgatory* (Oxford: Oxford University Press, 2009), 18.
5. William Manchester, *A World Lit Only by Fire: The Medieval Mind and the Renaissance* (1992) (New York: Sterling, 2014), 5–6.
6. Johan Huizinga, *The Autumn of the Middle Ages,* trans. Rodney J. Payton and Ulrich Mammitzsch (1923) (Chicago: University of Chicago Press, 1996), 163.
7. Barbara W. Tuchman, *A Distant Mirror: The Calamitous Fourteenth Century* (1978) (New York: Random House, 2014), 123–124.
8. Paul Gough, "Cultivating Dead Trees: The Legacy of Paul Nash as an Artist of Trauma, Wilderness and Recovery," *Journal of War and Culture Studies* 4.3 (2011): 6–7.
9. Mary Borden, "Where Is Jehovah?," in *Poetry of the First World War: An Anthology,* ed. Tim Kendall (Oxford: Oxford University Press, 2013), 76–77.
10. T. S. Eliot, *The Waste Land,* http://www.poetryfoundation.org/poems-and-poets/poems/detail/47311.
11. Ernest Hemingway, "Big Two-Hearted River: Part I," in *The First 49 Stories* (1939) (London: Jonathan Cape, 1972), 165.
12. F. Scott Fitzgerald, *The Great Gatsby* (1926) (London: Bloomsbury, 1994), 23.

13. Wilfrid Owen, "Insensibility," in Kendall, *Poetry of the First World War*, 155–156.

14. Charles Sorley, "When you see millions of the mouthless dead," in Kendall, *Poetry of the First World War*, 191.

15. Doris Zinkeisen, handwritten MS, n.d., N.D. IWM ARCH 29, Imperial War Museum, London.

16. Henry David Thoreau, *Walden and Civil Disobedience* (1854) (New York: Penguin, 1983), 135.

17. Irenaeus, *Against Heresies* 4.20.7.

18. *Dhammapada* 313.

19. Angela Kang and Mark Protosevich (panelists), "Zombies and the Undead," Austin Film Festival, October 30, 2015.

20. Manuel Gonzales, "All of Me," in *Miniature Wife and Other Stories*, 137.

21. Manohla Dargis, "Hard to Find Good Help? Not in This Little Town," *New York Times*, June 15, 2007, http://query.nytimes.com/gst/fullpage.html?res=9A06E6DF153FF936A25755C0A9619C8B63.

22. Robert Kirkman, *The Walking Dead*, vol. 1 (Berkeley: Image Comics, 2013), n.p.

23. Kang and Protosevich, "Zombies and the Undead."

24. Max Brooks, *The Zombie Survival Guide: Complete Protection from the Living Dead* (New York: Broadway, 2003), 16.

25. Manuel Gonzales, "Escape from the Mall," in *Miniature Wife and Other Stories*, 288–289.

26. Max Brooks, *World War Z: An Oral History of the Zombie War* (New York: Crown, 2006), 96–97, 102.

27. Roberto Aguirre-Sacasa, *Afterlife with Archie: vol. 1: Escape from Riverdale* (Pelham, NY: Archie Comics, 2014), n.p.

28. Aguirre-Sacasa, *Afterlife with Archie*, n.p.

29. Thích Nhất Hạnh, *The Miracle of Mindfulness: An Introduction to the Practice of Meditation* (Boston: Beacon Press, 1987), 14; Mark 4:23 and elsewhere.

30. Jane Austen and Seth Grahame-Smith, *Pride and Prejudice and Zombies* (Philadelphia: Quirk, 2009), 120.

31. William Blake Erickson and John Blanchar, "Apocalyptic Stress: Causes and Consequences of Stress at the End of the World," in *The Walking Dead Psychology: Psych of the Living Dead*, ed. Travis Langley (New York: Sterling, 2015), 133.

32. Brooks, *World War Z*, 13.
33. Kirkman, *Walking Dead*, vol. 1, n.p.
34. Cormac McCarthy, *The Road* (London: Picador, 2006), 57–58.
35. Kirkman, *Walking Dead*, vol. 1, n.p.
36. Pope Benedict XVI, "Feast of the Baptism of the Lord" (homily), January 13, 2008, Sistine Chapel, Rome, http://w2.vatican.va/content/benedict-xvi/en/homilies/2008/documents/hf_ben-xvi_hom_20080113_battesimo.html.
37. Aristotle, *De Anima* 2.3.
38. Genesis 1:27, NRSV.
39. Gilbert Ryle, *The Concept of Mind* (1949) (Chicago: University of Chicago Press, 2002).
40. Dawkins, "It's Time to Abandon the Irrational Concept of a Soul," https://richarddawkins.net/2015/01/its-time-to-abandon-the-irrational-concept-of-a-soul/.
41. Richard Dawkins, "Preface to the Paperback Edition," in *The God Delusion* (London: Black Swan, 2007), 21.
42. Brooks, *Zombie Survival Guide: Complete Protection from the Living Dead*, 76, 78.
43. Max Brooks, *The Zombie Survival Guide: Recorded Attacks* (New York: Three Rivers Press, 2009), n.p.
44. Robert Kirkman, *Marvel Zombies: The Complete Collection*, vol. 1 (New York: Marvel, 2015), n.p.
45. Kirkman, *Walking Dead*, vol. 1, n.p.
46. Henry Hanks, " 'Walking Dead' Finale: If Daryl Dies, We Riot," CNN, December 1, 2013, http://www.cnn.com/2013/11/29/showbiz/walking-dead-norman-reedus/; "The Transformation of Daryl Dixon," https://www.youtube.com/watch?v=yo-VOyEh5W0.
47. Hanks, " 'Walking Dead' Finale."
48. Desmond Tutu, *God Has a Dream: A Vision of Hope for Our Time* (New York: Image, 2004), 14.
49. Rowan William, *Tokens of Trust: An Introduction to Christian Belief* (Louisville, KY: Westminster John Knox, 2007), 42.
50. William, *Tokens of Trust*, 65.
51. "Sunday Morning With…," BBC Radio Scotland, January 31, 2016.
52. Jeremiah 22:1–5, NRSV.
53. My retelling of Luke 10:25–37.

54. Augustine, *De Doctrina Christiana* 1.28, 29.
55. John Donne, Meditation 17, http://www.online-literature.com/donne/409/.
56. Brooks, *World War Z*, 227.
57. Cullen Bunn, *Return of the Living Deadpool* (New York: Marvel, 2015), n.p.
58. Bunn, *Return of the Living Deadpool*, n.p.
59. George R. R. Martin, *A Clash of Kings: Book Two of A Song of Ice and Fire* (New York: Bantam, 1999), 945.

Chapter 2

1. Mark Protosevich, e-mail interview, April 16, 2016.
2. Max Brooks, *World War Z: An Oral History of the Zombie War* (New York: Crown, 2006), 125.
3. Brooks, *World War Z*, 127.
4. Karl Vick, "Sebastian Junger Says PTSD Is Our Fault," *Time*, May 29, 2016, http://time.com/4351069/memorial-day-2016-veterans-ptsd-sebastian-junger-tribe-book/.
5. Robert Kirkman, *The Walking Dead*, vol. 1 (Berkeley: Image Comics, 2013), n.p.
6. Kirkman, *Walking Dead*, vol. 1, n.p.
7. Max Brooks, *The Zombie Survival Guide: Complete Protection from the Living Dead* (New York: Broadway Books, 2003), 69, 99.
8. Brooks, *Zombie Survival Guide*, 159.
9. Jane Austen and Seth Grahame-Smith, *Pride and Prejudice and Zombies* (Philadelphia: Quirk, 2009), 14.
10. "Review: *Night of the Living Dead*," *Variety*, December 31, 1967, http://variety.com/1967/film/reviews/night-of-the-living-dead-1200421603/.
11. Robert Kirkman, "Marvel Zombies: Dead Days," in *Marvel Zombies: The Complete Collection*, vol. 1 (New York: Marvel, 2015), n.p.
12. J. Russell, *Book of the Dead: The Complete History of Zombie Cinema* (Surrey, England: FAB Press, 2005), 69.
13. Alain de Botton, *Religion for Atheists: A Non-believer's Guide to the Uses of Religion* (New York: Pantheon, 2012), 30.
14. Genesis 2:18, NRSV.
15. Psalm 13:1–2, NRSV.

16. Psalm 22:1–2, 11, NRSV.

17. Walter Brueggemann, *The Message of the Psalms* (Minneapolis: Augsburg, 1984), 52.

18. Psalm 25:16–21, NRSV.

19. Mark Protosevich, e-mail interview, April 16, 2016.

20. James L. Kugel, *How to Read the Bible: A Guide to Scripture, Then and Now* (New York: Free Press, 2007), 88.

21. Laura Prudom, "'Walking Dead' Producer Talks Latest Casualty: The Character WE Knew 'Is Dead,'" *Variety*, October 26, 2015, http://variety.com/2015/tv/news/glenn-walking-dead-alive-death-spoilers-1201626861/.

22. Jay L. Clendenin, "'Walking Dead': Steven Yeun's Glenn Is Beating Heart of AMC Series," *LA Times*, February 8, 2013, http://herocomplex.latimes.com/tv/walking-dead-steven-yeuns-glenn-is-beating-heart-of-amc-series/#/0.

23. Kat Rosenfield, "Try," *Entertainment Weekly*, March 23, 2015, http://www.ew.com/recap/the-walking-dead-season-5-episode-15.

24. Jürgen Moltmann, *History and the Triune God: Contributions to Trinitarian Theology* (New York: Crossroad, 1992), xii/xiii, 64.

25. John 13:34–35, NRSV.

26. John 15:12–15, NRSV; John 15:17, NRSV.

27. 1 John 3:11, 14b, NRSV.

28. Martin Luther King, Jr., *Strength to Love* (1963) (Philadelphia: Fortress, 1981), 52.

29. Roberto Aguirre-Sacasa, *Afterlife with Archie: vol. 1: Escape from Riverdale* (Pelham, NY: Archie Comics, 2014), n.p.

30. Matthew 18:15–17, NRSV.

31. Tom Wright, *Matthew for Everyone, Part 2* (Louisville, KY: Westminster John Knox, 2004), 36.

32. Romans 12:3–10, NRSV.

33. Rowan Williams, *Meeting God in Paul* (London: SPCK, 2015), 45–46.

34. In this and succeeding paragraphs, I offer my own retellings of some of the more familiar stories from the Desert tradition. Many collections of the Sayings of the Desert Mothers and Fathers exist. One of the most accessible is that edited by Benedicta Ward, *The Desert Fathers: Sayings of the Early Christian Monks* (New York: Penguin, 2003).

35. "Chapters of the Rule," chap. 1, Augustine's Rule, About Augustine, Augustine Spirituality, https://www1.villanova.edu/villanova/mission/campusministry/RegularSpiritualPractices/resources/spirituality/about/rule/chapters.html.

36. Thomas F. Martin, *Our Restless Heart: The Augustinian Tradition* (Maryknoll, NY: Orbis, 2003), 60.

37. Martin, *Our Restless Heart*, 1.3.

38. Martin, *Our Restless Heart*, 7.3.

39. Donald X. Burt, *Friendship and Society: An Introduction to Augustine's Practical Philosophy* (Grand Rapids, MI: Eerdmanns, 1999), 2, 4.

40. Samuel T. Lloyd III, "Practicing the Hope of the World," *Cathedral Voice*, September 2008, 1.

Chapter 3

1. Cormac McCarthy, *The Road* (London: Picador, 2006), 77.

2. Max Brooks, *The Zombie Survival Guide: Complete Protection from the Living Dead* (New York: Broadway Books, 2003), 155–156.

3. Brooks, *Zombie Survival Guide*, 163.

4. Kim Paffenroth, *Gospel of the Living Dead: George Romero's Visions of Hell on Earth* (Waco, TX: Baylor University Press, 2006), 84.

5. McCarthy, *Road*, 128–129.

6. Max Brooks, *World War Z: An Oral History of the Zombie War* (New York: Crown, 2006), 129.

7. McCarthy, *Road*, 110.

8. Dalton Ross, "And the Dead Shall Rise," *Entertainment Weekly*, February 13, 2015, 32.

9. Angela Kang and Mark Protosevich (panelists), "Zombies and the Undead," Austin Film Festival, October 30, 2015.

10. Jeremy Egner, "Ramsay Bolton of 'Game of Thrones' Is the Most Hated Man on TV," *New York Times*, April 20, 2016, http://www.nytimes.com/2016/04/24/arts/television/ramsay-bolton-of-game-of-thrones-is-the-most-hated-man-on-tv.html?_r=0.

11. Myles McNutt, "*Game of Thrones* Invites Kingsmoot Fever to Sweep the Globe," *A.V. Club*, May 1, 2016, http://www.avclub.com/tvclub/game-thrones-invites-kingsmoot-fever-sweep-globe-e-236099.

12. Dan Abnett, *The New Deadwardians* (New York: DC Comics, 2012), n.p.

13. Brooks, *World War Z*, 155–158.

14. Greg Garrett, *One Fine Potion: The Literary Magic of Harry Potter* (Waco, TX: Baylor University Press, 2010).

15. Rick Remender, *Uncanny Avengers* 18 (May 2014), n.p.

16. Romans 7:14–19, NRSV.

17. Alain de Botton, *Religion for Atheists: A Non-believer's Guide to the Uses of Religion* (New York: Pantheon, 2012), 82–83.

18. Rowan Williams, *Writing in the Dust: Reflections on 11th September and Its Aftermath* (London: Hodder and Stoughton, 2002), 23.

19. Mario Loyola, "*The Walking Dead*'s Political Philosophy," *National Review,* December 5, 2015, http://www.nationalreview.com/article/428043/walking-dead-zombies-philosophy.

20. Jane Mayer, *The Dark Side* (New York: Anchor, 2009), 174.

21. McCarthy, *Road,* 140.

22. McCarthy, *Road,* 34.

23. McCarthy, *Road,* 77.

24. Colt J. Blunt, "The Psychological Process and Cost of Killing in an Undead Wasteland," in *The Walking Dead Psychology: Psych of the Living Dead,* ed. Travis Langley (New York: Sterling, 2015), 79.

25. Justin Cronin, *The Passage* (Toronto: Doubleday Canada, 2010), 239.

26. Cronin, *Passage,* 240.

27. Brooks, *World War Z*, 107.

28. Brooks, *World War Z*, 116.

29. Brooks, *World War Z*, 166.

30. Scott Bader-Saye, *Following Jesus in a Culture of Fear* (Grand Rapids, MI: Brazos, 2007), 118–119.

31. Manuel Gonzales, "Escape from the Mall," in *The Miniature Wife and Other Stories* (New York: Riverhead, 2013), 298.

32. McCarthy, *Road,* 127.

33. McCarthy, *Road,* 151.

34. Thomas Hobbes, *Leviathan,* ed. Richard Tuck (Cambridge: Cambridge University Press, 1991), 63.

35. McCarthy, *Road,* 257.

36. Bertrand Russell, *War: The Offspring of Fear* (London: Union of Democratic Control, 1915), 10.

37. Russell, *War*, 10, 3, 11.

38. Thomas Merton, *Seeds of Contemplation* (1961) (Wheathampstead, England: Anthony Clarke, 1972), 86.

39. Merton, *Seeds of Contemplation*, 138.

40. Jean Bethke Elshtain, "Augustine," in *The Blackwell Companion to Political Theology*, ed. Peter Scott and William T. Cavanaugh (Oxford: Blackwell, 2007), 45.

41. Wendy Murray Zoba, "Civic Housekeeping: Jean Elshtain on Mothering and Other Duties," *Christian Century*, May 18, 2004, http://findarticles.com/p/articles/mi_m1058/is_10_120/ai_102140728/?tag=content;col1.

42. Frank Herbert, *Dune* (1965) (London: Hodder and Stoughton, 1968), 19.

43. Rowan Williams, "The Government Needs to Know How Afraid People Are," *New Statesman*, June 13, 2011, 5.

44. Bader-Saye, *Following Jesus in a Culture of Fear*, 33.

45. William E. Gladstone, *War in China: Speech of the Rt. Hon. W. E. Gladstone, MP, Mar 3 1857* (London: Rivingtons, 1857), 36.

46. Robert Kolker, "The Politics of Being Afraid," *New York*, May 21, 2005, http://nymag.com/nymetro/news/people/columns/intelligencer/9620/.

47. Bader-Saye, *Following Jesus in a Culture of Fear*, 27.

48. John Gray, *Black Mass: Apocalyptic Religion and the Death of Utopia* (London: Penguin, 2008), 139.

49. Reinhold Niebuhr, *The Irony of American History* (1952) (Chicago: University of Chicago Press, 2008), 40.

50. Mayer, *Dark Side*, 132.

51. Niebuhr, *Irony of American History*, 5.

52. McCarthy, *Road*, 259.

53. Niebuhr, *Irony of American History*, 5.

54. Bader-Saye, *Following Jesus in a Culture of Fear*, 102.

55. Roberto Aguirre-Sacasa, *Afterlife with Archie: vol. 1: Escape from Riverdale* (Pelham, NY: Archie Comics, 2014), n.p.

56. Aguirre-Sacasa, *Afterlife with Archie*, n.p.

57. Aguirre-Sacasa, *Afterlife with Archie*, n.p.

58. His Holiness the Dalai Lama, *Ethics for the New Millennium* (New York: Riverhead, 1999), 131.

59. The Benedictine Rule, chap. 53.
60. Stanley Hauerwas, *The Peaceable Kingdom: A Primer in Christian Ethics* (Notre Dame, IN: University of Notre Dame Press, 1983), xvii.
61. Martin Luther King, Jr., *Strength to Love* (New York: Harper and Row, 1963), 53.
62. Dalai Lama, *Ethics for the New Millennium*, 201.
63. John Howard Yoder, *The Politics of Jesus* (Grand Rapids, MI: Eerdmanns, 1996), 96.
64. Bader-Saye, *Following Jesus in a Culture of Fear*, 67.
65. Simon Spurrier, *Marvel Zombies* 3 (October 2015), n.p.
66. Simon Spurrier, *Marvel Zombies* 1 (August 2015), n.p.
67. Spurrier, *Marvel Zombies* 1, n.p.
68. Martin Luther King, Jr., "I've Been to the Mountaintop (April 3, 1968)," American Rhetoric, http://www.americanrhetoric. com/speeches/mlkivebeentothemountaintop.htm. In an earlier sermon on the Good Samaritan, Dr. King called this a dangerous altruism. Perhaps be believed "unselfishness" was easier to understand. Or perhaps he came to believe that the connotation of "altruism" as a generosity or gift associated with the wealthy relieved some of his listeners of their responsibility. Martin Luther King, Jr., "On Being a Good Neighbor," in *Strength to Love*, 33.
69. McCarthy, *Road*, 280–281.
70. McCarthy, *Road*, 282–284.

Chapter 4

1. Ezekiel 37:1–14, NRSV.
2. James F. Kugel, *How to Read the Bible: A Guide to Scripture, Then and Now* (New York: Free Press, 2007), 656.
3. Bart Ehrman, *The New Testament: A Historical Introduction to the Early Christian Writings* (New York: Oxford University Press, 2004), 491.
4. John Gray, *Black Mass: Apocalyptic Religion and the Death of Utopia* (London: Penguin, 2008), 2.
5. Jonathan Kirsch, *A History of the End of the World: How the Most Controversial Book in the Bible Changed the Course of Western Civilization* (New York: HarperOne, 2006), 5.

6. Raymond E. Brown, *An Introduction to the New Testament* (New York: Doubleday, 1997), 773.
7. Augustine, *City of God* 22.7, 719.
8. M. Eugene Boring gently tries to explain that the Revelation is a pastoral letter to Asian first-century Christians confronted by religious and political difficulties from a Christian prophet who chose to use familiar (at least to him) apocalyptic symbols and stories. See Boring, *Revelation*, IBC (Louisville, KY: John Knox, 1989), 1.
9. Nicholas Guyatt, *Have a Nice Doomsday: Why Millions of Americans Are Looking Forward to the End of the World* (New York: Harper Perennial, 2007), 69.
10. Daniel Wojcik, *The End of the World as We Know It: Faith, Fatalism, and Apocalypse in America* (New York: New York University Press, 1997), 4.
11. Adela Yarbro Collins, *Crisis and Catharsis: The Power of the Apocalypse* (Philadelphia: Westminster, 1984), 156.
12. Richard Matheson, *I Am Legend* (1954) (New York: Tor, 1995), 3.
13. Matheson, *I Am Legend*, 159.
14. Matheson, *I Am Legend* (New York: Tom Doherty Associates, 2007), 103.
15. Cormac McCarthy, *Blood Meridian: Or the Evening Redness in the West* (New York: Random House, 1985), 253.
16. Geoff Johns, *Blackest Night* (New York: DC Comics, 2010), n.p.
17. David Sims and Lenika Cruz, "*The Walking Dead* and the Cheapness of Death," *Atlantic*, April 4, 2016, http://www.theatlantic.com/entertainment/archive/2016/04/walking-dead-season-six-episode-16-recap-last-day-earth/476349/http://www.theatlantic.com/entertainment/archive/2016/04/walking-dead-season-six-episode-16-recap-last-day-earth/476349/.
18. Roberta Smith, "For Rothko, It Wasn't All Black Despair," *New York Times*, March 6, 1994, http://www.nytimes.com/1994/03/06/arts/gallery-view-for-rothko-it-wasn-t-all-black-despair.html.
19. Charles Sorley, "When You See Millions of the Mouthless Dead," in *Poetry of the First World War: An Anthology*, ed. Tim Kendall (Oxford: Oxford University Press, 2013), 191.
20. Walker Percy, "The Man on the Train," in *The Message in the Bottle* (1975) (New York: Picador, 2000), 83.

21. Revelation 11:15–19, 12:1–2, NRSV.
22. Travis Langley, "Introduction: The Uncanny Valley of the Shadow of Death," in *The Walking Dead Psychology: Psych of the Living Dead,* ed. Travis Langley (New York: Sterling, 2015), 2.
23. J. R. R. Tolkien, "On Fairy Stories," in *Tales from the Perilous Realm* (New York: Houghton Mifflin, 2008), 384.
24. Johns, *Blackest Night,* n.p.
25. Julian of Norwich, *Revelations of Divine Love,* trans. Elizabeth Spearing (New York: Penguin, 1998), 155.
26. Evan Calder-Williams, *Combined and Uneven Apocalypse: Luciferian Marxism* (Winchester, England: Zero Books, 2010), 5.
27. Calder-Williams, *Combined and Uneven Apocalypse,* 8.
28. Mark Protosevich, e-mail interview, April 16, 2016.
29. Manuel Gonzales, "Escape from the Mall," in *The Miniature Wife and Other Stories* (New York: Riverhead, 2013), 300.

Conclusion

1. John Russo, "Foreword: Why Don't They Die?," in *The Walking Dead Psychology: Psych of the Living Dead,* ed. Travis Langley (New York: Sterling, 2015), xv.

INDEX